SIMPLE PRUNING

2.50

Muriel Johnson.
Fieldhead
Mayfield

Staff

SIMPLE PRUNING

N. CATCHPOLE

R.H.S. GOLD MEDALLIST

LONDON
W. H. & L. COLLINGRIDGE LTD
TRANSATLANTIC ARTS
NEW YORK

PUBLISHED BY

W. & H. L. COLLINGRIDGE LTD
*2–10 Tavistock Street, Covent Garden, W.C.2
and in the United States of America by*
TRANSATLANTIC ARTS INC.
*Forest Hills, New York 17, N.Y., U.S.A.
Made and printed in Great Britain by
Morrison & Gibb Ltd, London & Edinburgh*

FIRST EDITION 1930
SECOND EDITION 1934
REPRINTED 1936
REPRINTED 1939
REPRINTED 1941
REPRINTED 1944
THIRD EDITION 1946
REPRINTED 1947
REPRINTED 1948
REPRINTED 1949

INTRODUCTION

In presenting a third edition of this book, I would like to make some apology for what may appear at a first glance a somewhat lengthy discourse in the first two chapters.

As a student, and in turn an employee and employer, I have always found clear-cut gardening instructions unsatisfactory. In the early days of training in different nurseries I always liked to be told why I was doing a particular job, and the results which were likely to accrue from such work.

I well remember when as a student at the R.H.S. Gardens, Wisley, I received my first instructions in pruning. The subject was the apple, and the lesson merely told how to do the work, without giving reasons, and most of the students I think left the lecture without feeling much wiser. Ever since I always wanted, if possible, to know the 'reason why', and in after years, when it has become my turn to give instructions, I have always tried to be as explicit as possible.

In successful pruning it is very necessary to know a certain amount about your subject's mode of living. In particular it is essential to understand the factors which influence vigour, because pruning is so very much related to and governed by degree of growth. It is for these reasons that the opening pages deal with theoretical information which is of importance if the subject is to be properly understood.

I would like to make special mention here of the change over in ideas about successful apple pruning. Some fifteen years ago I planted an orchard mainly of apples and pears, and including about three acres of cordons and about 2000 bush trees. This is but a small commercial orchard, but it is of such a size that it is possible for me to prune every tree (with assistance) each winter. I have experimented with varying methods of pruning, especially during the last five years, when activities with flowering plants have been practically excluded, and it has been possible to observe the reactions on every tree. The result of these observations are condensed in the text of this book.

I would like very much to express my appreciation of the magnificent work done by our research stations at East Malling and Long Ashton and the practical manner in which they have helped commercial fruit growers. The real assistance and the information which they have given in the past has been of very real help to progressive growers, and the practical results when fully tried and proved can be handed on, not as first-hand knowledge, but as proven material which is the result of the study of many people.

N. CATCHPOLE

DITCHLING
SUSSEX, 1946.

CONTENTS

LIST OF ILLUSTRATIONS

CHAPTER ONE

THE PURPOSE OF PRUNING

THE process of pruning has been aptly described as 'the removal of superfluities'. It plays an important part in the successful cultivation of nearly all trees, shrubs and climbing plants, besides many other types, including practically all varieties of fruit. The superfluities of plants are numerous, and consequently pruning takes several forms, and includes not only the cutting away of wood, dead or alive, but the pinching out of young shoots, the removal of faded blossoms and seed pods, the thinning of flowers and fruits, and the cutting away of various portions of root systems.

All this may sound artificial, and the beginner may well argue that a plant is best left as Nature intended, but the answer lies in the fact that the lives of most plants in gardens are unnatural. Nature intends that a plant should live merely in order that it may reproduce itself in as great quantities as possible through the medium of its capacity to yield an abundance of flowers and eventually seeds. The horticulturist, however, desires to regulate the maturation of his plants in an artificial manner. This is because it is not always wise to allow a plant to develop naturally, since unwanted portions of it may develop at the expense of those which are essential from the cultivator's point of view.

In many instances a plant is grown for the beauty of its flower alone. Where this is the case, the production of seed has to be checked, in order that the future energy may be thrown into the production of further quantities of flowers. On the other hand, where fruit is required, it may be necessary to restrict the number of flowers, in order that the quantity of fruits produced may be reasonably small. In other instances, certain parts of trees must be made to develop at the expense of others, and some of them must be so regulated as to supply not only a crop of fruit for the current season, but also a generous amount of growth which will provide next year's supply.

Pruning, then, does not consist of taking the shears or sécateurs into the garden and indulging in the time-honoured practice of 'trimming to shape', but is a science which in one way and another controls the building up and the regulation of development in plants in order that they shall fulfil to the utmost the purpose for which they were planted.

Any amount of time, energy and money may be spent on purchasing good stock from reliable sources, in thorough soil preparation and in correct planting, yet for those subjects which require it there is no substitute for proper pruning, and unless it is carried out real success cannot follow.

There is probably no branch of horticulture that is more misapplied and less understood, and there is ample evidence of this statement in gardens throughout the country. Correct pruning may easily spell the difference between success and failure, yet many people go to infinite pains to get the best out of their gardens but neglect to give their consideration to this important question.

The work itself is fascinating, and those who take the trouble to study plants and their individual requirements in this direction will be more than repaid for their trouble.

The Main Reasons for Pruning.—For those who are anxious to gain some knowledge of this subject, it is important first of all to consider why it is necessary, and also the main principles embodied in its practice.

The chief reasons for pruning may be most easily considered if they are divided into four headings : (*a*) pruning to maintain shape ; (*b*) removal of dead, weak, unhealthy and overcrowded growth ; (*c*) removal of unnecessary growth, fruit and flowers ; (*d*) conservation and direction of energy. As these matters are of importance, they must be considered in some detail.

A. Pruning to Maintain Shape and Even Balance of Growth within Required Dimensions

The importance of keeping plants within bounds speaks for itself. It all too frequently occurs that the stronger growing inhabitants of a shrub border which are often the less choice, are allowed to extend beyond their allotted portion to the detriment of their smaller growing neighbours. The same sort of thing happens in the rock garden and in the orchard, and whilst the trouble may in some measure be due to injudicious planning at planting time, the difficulty may be overcome by correct pruning. What must be avoided at all costs is the method employed in so many gardens of giving shrubs an annual trimming to give what the operator considers a neat appearance, because this destroys individuality, and in many instances also includes the removal of flowering wood. It is a simple matter, and frequently a beneficial one, to restrict or to reduce size of any shrub or tree when the process of pruning is fully understood.

Many flowering trees and shrubs, as well as certain varieties of apples, pears and bush fruits require careful attention in order to prevent the formation of a lop-sided specimen. The important work here lies in correct treatment in the very early stages of the tree's development. The foundation of a good tree, and of many bad ones too, I fear, is laid down in the nursery, which shows the importance of buying from reliable firms.

The retention of an even balance of growth has a further and most important bearing which at first may not be fully apparent. It concerns the relationships in growth between roots and the upper portions of a plant, and none can hope to become proficient in the art of pruning unless the full significance of the question is grasped. The principles involved are of considerable importance in successful tree fruit growing, and may also be extended to other subjects.

Roots and Top Growth.—It should first be pointed out that there are two principal types of roots produced by plants, which affect their growth. The first type is known as fibrous, and, as the name suggests, roots of this kind are numerous as well as fine, and are generally compact in their growth. They tend towards the production of moderate vigour in the portions of plants above ground, and encourage flowering and fruitfulness. They are produced comparatively near the surface of the soil, and appear more naturally and in greater abundance on light than on heavy soils. Incidentally, well-grown nursery specimens should lift almost entirely with fibrous roots, which, in the case of some subjects, are so fine as to carry a large 'ball' of soil with them. This is an acquisition which assists successful transplanting, and is particularly essential in the case of ever-green subjects.

The second type is known as a tap root. Roots of this class are strong growing, and as a rule penetrate downwards to a considerable depth. They are productive of strong, coarse growth above ground, which is associated with unfruitfulness, and they are therefore generally to be considered as undesirable except in the case of strong growing trees used for ornamental or screening purposes.

These two root systems are described on account of their relation to the general vigour and habit of plants. The full understanding as to comparative vigour is essential to the practice of successful pruning, and must be considered further.

Other Factors Influencing Vigour.—There are one or two further factors which influence growth and will have to be taken into account. In the first place heavy soils are more likely to produce strong growth than light ones. This is in some measure due to the fact that the texture of a soil containing a high proportion of clay or silt tends to check the production of fibrous roots. For example, the tiny rootlets produced by most rhododendrons are unable to penetrate into a stiff clay medium, and consequently only the stronger rooting kinds are selected for such soils. It must further be borne in mind that for the most part heavy soils are naturally more rich in elementary plant foods, and also are more retentive of moisture. Both of these factors are conducive to strong growth. Lastly, situation has to be considered. It is necessary to grasp the fact that although plants always strive to grow towards light, and in some cases grow spindly in their efforts to do so, light actually retards growth. Plants in the shade grow more strongly than those planted where they are fully exposed to the sun. This fact is always proved when an over-crowded shrub border or even an orchard is thinned by a grubbing out of a proportion of specimens. One would expect that the trees retained would immediately respond to the added space around them with increased vigour. Actually the reverse is the case, owing to the extra amount of light made available, and strong growth will only be renewed if encouragement is given in the shape of a nitrogenous manure.

It must also be appreciated that different varieties of the

same species vary very considerably in vigour. For example, roses such as Emma Wright, General McArthur and Golden Gleam are not nearly so strong growing as Betty Uprichard, George Dickson and Shot Silk, yet they are all Hybrid Tea Roses. The variety of Mock Orange known as Lemoinei is much more compact than its more vigorous brother, which is called grandiflorus. Amongst apples there is considerable diversity in strength of growth, frequently causing much perplexity to their owners. The classic example of over-exuberance is almost always Bramley's Seedling, whilst at the other end of the scale are to be found such varieties as Ribston Pippin and Worcester Pearmain, which are more compact and moderate in habit. It would be possible to continue through the whole range of plants which at some time or another require pruning, and I would like to stress the importance of bearing this varying varietal degree of growth in mind when pruning time arrives.

Effect of Vigour on Usefulness.—The main factors which influence vigour in all types of plants have now been briefly outlined. It remains to be explained what is the relationship between vigour and pruning. It is impossible to overemphasise the importance of appreciating how the one influences the other. The manner in which pruning is carried out has a very marked effect on vigour. Vigour in its turn is the main factor which governs the efficiency and therefore the usefulness of roses, shrubs and all kinds of fruit trees. It is important to bear in mind that at this stage I am only generalising, but the principle remains in all classes of plants where pruning is practised.

In general terms it would be correct to say that excessive vigour is not consistent with maximum flower production, and it obviously follows that it cannot result in heavy fruit production. Such growth is most frequently to be found in gardens on specimens which are not growing upon their own roots; that is to say, it has been necessary to propagate them by means of either budding or grafting them on alien stocks. In some cases these stocks have a more vigorous rooting system than is actually required. But it may also in some cases be experienced in plants growing upon their own roots.

On the other hand, with stunted growth where there is

obviously insufficient vigour, a set of conditions must be studied which generally result in very inefficient flower and fruit production. In flowering plants, blossoms will be few and very small, and in fruit trees there will be a tendency to produce crops only every second or even every third year. The tree is in such an exhausted state that it takes two years to recover sufficiently before producing another crop, and even then this will be small and of poor quality.

To put the situation quite briefly, there are numerous varying factors which influence vigour in practically all classes of plants. Degree of vigour affects quality, quantity and regularity of flower and fruit production. To some extent strength of growth may be regulated by the manner of pruning adopted.

I would like to emphasise the extreme importance of grasping the general principles briefly outlined in the following paragraph, because they are all important if the subject of pruning is to be thoroughly understood.

Pruning and Vigour.—Before making an endeavour to describe how to prune different subjects, it is necessary to illustrate the precise results which accrue from that operation. The fundamental fact to be borne in mind is that the harder a plant is pruned the more vigorously it will continue to grow, and, conversely, the more lightly it is cut, the less will be the subsequent vigour. This is a most important fact, and must be duly borne in mind whenever the knife or shears are put into use. For example, a privet hedge can be built up far more quickly and effectively by cutting it hard back soon after it is first planted, and by continuing to remove from 6 inches to 1 foot of top growth in subsequent seasons. If it be merely lightly clipped the resultant growth will not be nearly so strong or so thick. If one leading shoot of a currant bush or apple tree be cut back, and another be only lightly pruned, the former will produce much stronger growth than the latter during the following season. The same remark applies to all woody subjects, and can be extended to herbaceous and annual plants. Consider, for example, a delphinium and an antirrhinum. As soon as the first beauty of flower is fading, seed formation will have begun. The more rigorously old flowering stems and seed pods are cut away, the more vigorous will be the resultant

Two contrasted types of root stock. On the left is the root system of a young crab apple showing thongy roots which encourage vigorous growth. Below is the far more fibrous root system of a dwarfing Paradise apple stock.

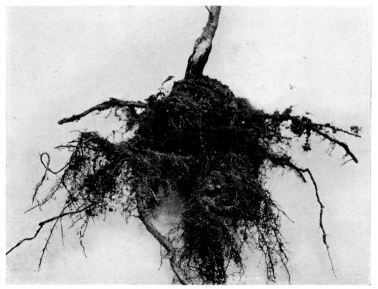

Root pruning an overvigorous young tree which has been lifted for the purpose.

Curbing the vigour of a fruit tree by removing two half-rings of bark around the main trunk.

Removing suckers from a wall-trained plum tree.

secondary growth, with a corresponding increase in the quality and quantity of the second crop of flowers. In each case a portion of the plant which would otherwise have absorbed a considerable amount of energy for its maturation has been removed, with the result that the same energy has been reserved for more useful channels.

Root Pruning.—It has already been intimated that it is possible indirectly to control the vigour, and consequent fruitfulness, of plants by manipulating the root system in an artificial manner. It is well known that by adding plant stimulants in the form of manures, either dug into the ground or applied as a mulch, we may increase vigour. In just the same way it is possible to curb excessive growth by means of checking the plant's powers of absorbing moisture and elementary foods. This is brought about by the process known as 'root pruning'. It consists principally in cutting away the stronger growing or 'tap' roots, which have already been described. The worst offending of these roots are generally those which penetrate directly downwards into the subsoil, where they come into contact with an abundant water supply, and consequently result in the production of rank, soft and sappy growth. When these strong growing roots are carefully severed they often produce a number of smaller roots, which frequently take the form desired—namely, fibrous. Root pruning, therefore, is a big factor in the control of vigour, and is a very important operation.

Ringing or Ring-barking.—Yet another method of reducing excessive vigour is provided by the operation known as Ringing or Ring-barking. In order to understand how this method works, it is necessary to appreciate quite briefly how a plant lives and feeds. Put as concisely as I can manage, this is what happens. Roots obtain from the soil certain raw plant foods, which are drawn in solution from the soil. There is a process of selection so that the plant only takes what it requires from that which is available. This solution passes up the centre or inner parts of the trunk and branches to the leaves, where with the addition of carbon taken from the air (in the form of carbon dioxide, the oxygen being returned to the atmosphere) and by the aid of light, complicated and completed plant foods are manufactured. These foods are transported

B

to all parts of the plant, a large proportion going to the roots by way of the outside layers of the branches and stems; that is to say, in the layers closely beneath the bark, and outside the woody part through which the raw foods travelled upwards. Ringing consists of removing a strip of bark right round the girth of the trunk, not necessarily all in one plane, but in two semicircles which are opposite to each other and about 6 inches apart. The separated half-circles check the flow of food back to the roots and so have a determined effect in the reduction of vigour. It is a method most frequently used on well-established fruit trees which have consistently refused to moderate their vigour and which must be brought to heel before they will start bearing.

Incidentally, a similar effect is often produced in Nature on apple trees when canker attacks occur. On strong growing trees single branches may often be attacked, and whilst the wound is small it will be noticed that vigour is reduced and fruitfulness brought about. But if the disease spreads right round the branch it is certain to die. A practical point that arises is therefore the necessity of regular examination of all kinds of ties used to support stems or branches, especially wire ones which are used on some types of labels. If the cutting-in process goes too far the portion above the tie will be lost.

It will thus be observed that the maintenance of an even balance of growth between roots and branches is entirely within the hands of the cultivator. By means of judicious root pruning, and careful discrimination in the amount of wood removed, size, vigour, fruitfulness and comparative age can be manipulated at will.

By such means it is possible also to rejuvenate old and worn-out fruit trees, as well as old specimens of flowering trees, such as rhododendrons, lilacs and laburnums. Worn-out branches and stems are cut back, thereby encouraging fresh young growths which maintain their vigour for a season or two, and then settle down to renewed fruitfulness.

Although the principles which have been discussed are simple, their knowledge embodies the basis of successful pruning.

B. The Removal of Dead, Weak, Unhealthy and Overcrowded Growths

It is important that the growth of plants should never be allowed to become overcrowded. It is frequently necessary to open out certain specimens, particularly thickly growing ornamental shrubs as well as bush and standard fruit trees. This enables sun and air to reach every remaining branch and shoot, ripening the wood and plumping up the buds.

The extent to which such thinning should be done depends to some extent upon the vigour of the tree. As previously explained, strong growing trees require light pruning only, whilst those which are slow growing benefit from severe treatment. In any case, it is always advisable to remove unhealthy growth, and almost without exception those shoots which are misshapen and straggly. Dead, diseased and insect-infested wood should be removed and burned before pests have time to spread to susceptible neighbours.

The commonly occurring coral-spot fungus, which is often seen on pea boughs, can only enter a plant through dead wood; but it has been shown that, once established, it spreads to the living tissues, and often causes considerable damage. This frequently occurs with currant bushes.

In the orchard it is important to remove damaged wood of any kind, such as scars caused through clumsy pruning and wood broken whilst gathering fruit, because such wounds are an excellent means for the introduction of apple canker disease. The same remarks apply to branches which have been badly infected with woolly aphis (American blight). If you have had a bad attack of scab on your apples or pears, make sure that all affected young shoots are removed, otherwise there will be a reinfestation the following year, and canker is almost certain to gain access. This disease is never far away when scab is not controlled. The presence of the latter is obvious during the growing season, causing blotches on the leaves and spotting and cracking of the fruit. In the dormant stage when entire removal is essential its presence may be detected by blistering and cracking of the bark on young shoots.

The necessity for the removal of weak growths speaks for

itself. Such wood is not productive of the best results, whilst its removal facilitates the ripening of remaining wood. This ripening is a big factor towards the health and well-being of plants, rendering them less susceptible to the attacks of insect pests and fungus diseases. It further renders woody growth less liable to injury by frost. It is important to remember, too, that well-ripened wood, besides being more healthy, is also productive of the best results and provides the strongest flowers and finest fruits. Generally speaking, in all cases where young wood is being removed on account of disease, it is better to cut it right away, and the same remark applies to thin and overcrowded shoots. It is seldom that any advantage arises from thin wood which has been shortened. In the case of a branch attacked high up, it may be possible to shorten it back into sound wood at a point where a young shoot is pointing in the desired direction.

C. Removal of Unnecessary Growth, Fruit and Flowers

The last point under consideration deals with the timely removal of unnecessary young growth, fruit and flowers with the idea of throwing the plant's energies into the most profitable channels. This is a most important form of pruning, which covers a wide field, and which should be practised wherever possible. It has been said that all pruning should be done with the thumb and forefinger, which means that the observant pruner removes all superfluous growths before they have attained any appreciable size, thus retaining all the available energy of the plant for the building up of the remaining portions. This is, in a measure, true, for much can be done in this way. It is obviously better to remove unrequired parts of a plant as early as possible, but at the same time instances abound where growths obtain considerable dimensions before they can be regarded as superfluous, in which cases the knife, sécateurs or even saw have to be used.

Stopping or Pinching.—The types of pruning which can be done with thumb and forefinger as referred to above, include 'stopping' or 'pinching' and 'disbudding'. The former two terms are more or less analogous, and represent the simplest form of pruning done in this way. Stopping is a method employed to induce a bushy habit; that is to say, the growing tip is removed in order to encourage the more immediate formation of side shoots. Typical examples are to be found in antirrhinum, carnation and chrysanthemum. It is sometimes necessary to carry out the operation twice on the same plant in order to obtain the required number of shoots, hence the terms 'first' and 'second stopping'. Ridge cucumbers and trailing marrows are stopped early in their development in order to provide shoots which may be laid out in all directions. They would again be stopped at each growing point when they had filled the space provided for them. The frame melon would have three distinct stoppings. First, to provide four shoots; second, to stop those shoots when they reached the corners of the frame, and to encourage the formation of fruiting side shoots or 'laterals'; and third, the stopping of these laterals at three or four leaves beyond the fruit if you have been sufficiently lucky to set it.

Various forms of stopping are employed upon tomatoes. Out of doors, according to the site or season, plants should be stopped at one leaf above the third or fourth truss, although I have seen plants ripening five good trusses in favoured positions. Side shoots are pinched out. Indoor crops are treated in varying ways. Some growers think that some sort of check should be given to upward growth when four trusses have formed. That is to say, as soon as they can fairly see and handle a leaf above the fourth truss they pinch out the small growing tip at this leaf. I think that this stopping does accelerate the maturing of the bottom trusses, and in the meantime about a fortnight later a strong young shoot will spring from the base of the topmost leaf retained, and will be trained on upwards to produce two or three more trusses of fruit. Other growers stop at two leaves above the sixth truss, and train out a side shoot on either side, each to provide one more truss of fruit. A good plan for amateurs who may consider the production of some good late fruit as more important than total weight, is to remove altogether the fourth and fifth trusses and to retain the sixth. The first three trusses provide early fruit which is used before the outdoor crop is ready, whilst the sixth ripens when the latter is finished.

Disbudding.—Disbudding is a somewhat loose term, which covers a variety of methods of pruning. It is naturally associated with the removal of flower buds of a secondary size in order that the stronger ones may develop more fully, and is employed upon such subjects as roses, chrysanthemums and carnations. The term also relates to an important principle governing the successful cultivation of peaches and nectarines, as well as some flowering shrubs, which will be fully dealt with later on. Another method used to advantage with herbaceous plants and all shrubs which should be pruned to the ground every year consists in the thinning out or disbudding of young shoots produced in spring. Although the resultant number of flowers may be reduced in quantity, this is more than compensated by the quality, and a much finer display assured. I am quite certain that this simple operation is seldom practised in the herbaceous border, which is a great pity, because it gives such fine results, and incidentally is of assistance in the staking and tying problem. Such subjects as delphiniums, phloxes, lupins, Michaelmas daisies, sidalceas and gypsophilas should certainly be treated. In some cases the advantage goes further, and may even save the life of the plant. This is frequently found where subjects are liable to set heavy crops of seed, and the most striking example is *Salvia turkestanica*, not a common plant, perhaps, but one of the most beautiful. If its shoots are not thinned it exhausts itself and dies. Anchusas sometimes behave in the same way.

Among shrubs, those which flower on wood of the current season's growth, and which are cut back to ground level each year or even back to a framework of old wood, will benefit from a thinning of resultant young shoots. Examples are *Hydrangea paniculata*, *Spiræa Anthony Waterer*, *Buddleia variabilis* and its varieties and the so-called hardy fuchsias such as *F. gracilis* and *F. macrostemma*.

Thinning.—It is well known that it is advisable to thin heavy crops of apples, pears, peaches, gooseberries and other fruits. Not only do the individual fruits which remain become much finer, but exhaustion of the parent tree is prevented, which will in some measure affect the bearing of the next and, perhaps, the following season. The skilled cultivator carries the process even further by restricting the number of flowers produced by thinning or cutting out the number of fruiting spurs, especially on stunted trees in full bearing.

The process of thinning is doubly carried out upon grape vines, for not only are the berries in each bunch reduced in number, but also each rod should not be allowed to carry more than a certain number of bunches, according to the area of glass covered.

D. Conservation and Direction of Energy

The last point dealing with the reasons for pruning is to some extent already covered by the previous headings. For example, the maintenance of shape in plants is frequently brought about by the removal of certain portions in order that others, which are more necessary, may receive the benefit of the converted energy for developing more fully. Such an instance is represented by the 'stopping' of chrysanthemums, carnations and other plants. The leading shoot is pinched out in order to encourage a bushy habit, and very frequently a second 'stopping' is practised a few weeks later in order to increase the number of leading shoots even further. Such operations are best guided by observation and common sense, and the cultivator must mould his plants according to requirements.

Prevention of Seed Formation.—Most important, however, is the prevention of formation of any part of the plant which is unnecessary. It is very probable that more beauty is lost to gardens every year through failure to observe this simple rule than through any other cause. In the case of all seed-bearing plants which are not actually being grown for the production of fruit or seed, it is most important that all faded flowers should be removed as soon as possible. Nothing exhausts a plant more than that it should be allowed to bear seed. Energy which would otherwise be utilised in the formation of further crops of flowers is wasted. This point should most particularly be borne in mind in the case of all hardy annuals, bedding plants, such as antirrhinums, violas, pansies, wallflowers, dahlias and polyanthus, together with a host of other subjects, including many herbaceous plants which either have a continuous season of blooming, or else two flowering periods, as is the case with delphiniums and lupins. Lastly, such woody subjects as rhododendrons, azaleas, heaths, roses, laburnums, lilacs and the like, which require all available energy for the formation either of next year's flowering wood or for secondary growth which produces a later crop of flowers.

This form of pruning is, above all, important with annuals. If left to seed, their beauty is fleeting and lasts but a few weeks, whereas if seed pods are systematically removed they will remain in flower for the greater part of the summer. It has been mentioned before that the object of plant life is to reproduce itself. In the case of annuals, therefore, which have but a very short existence, the tendency is for rapid and early seed formation, and although the work of removing seed pods may be regarded by some as being laborious, the time spent is more than well repaid by the continued beauty consequently produced. A packet of annual seeds costs less than a single bedding plant, so that the extra attention required for this simple process is easily covered by the saving in initial expenditure. These remarks apply particularly to annual chrysanthemums, nasturtiums, eschscholtzias, linarias, bartonia, coreopsis, annual lupin, godetia, mignonette, phacelia, clarkia, poppies, marigolds and china asters, whilst with antirrhinums a continual display from June to October can be guaranteed following an application of this principle.

The same practice is recommended for a host of other plants. It is wise to prevent seed formation in such subjects as hyacinths, tulips, daffodils, gladioli, irises, lilacs, tigridias and the like. It is not so much a question of securing succession of flower as the conservation of energy for next year's bulb or corm. Again, in the kitchen garden it is unwise to allow rhubarb to run up to seed, whilst onions can be prevented from doing the same by cutting the flowering stem through where it is solid, just below the head of flowers. Incidentally, it is unwise to allow any vegetables to 'bolt' to seed, as the flower is useless and the ground impoverished if they are left for any length of time.

Gunneras are grown in damp situations or in the wild garden for the attractiveness of their immense foliage. The flowering spikes, which have no ornamental value, should be removed as soon as they appear from the crown of the plant.

Removal of Suckers.—The next point to be considered is the removal of sucker growths produced in fruit trees, roses and many ornamental shrubs. It is unfortunate that many of these subjects cannot be grown upon their own roots, owing to the fact that most of them cannot be kept true to type if raised from seed. Some cannot be rooted from cuttings or layers, whilst others which do root under such treatment are unsatisfactory. Such plants are, therefore, either budded or grafted upon alien stocks. Many of these stocks—as, for example, the rugosa, dog-briar and other rose species frequently used for roses—have a habit of throwing up sucker growths, which should be removed immediately. They should be cut back some distance into the ground, preferably as far back as there is any tendency for upward growth, or the trouble will shortly recur. One frequently hears the complaint that a certain rose bush has 'reverted to the wild'. This is sheer nonsense, for all that has happened is that the stock has been allowed to grow up and starve the original out of existence. This accounts for the fact that *Rosa rugosa* is frequently seen flourishing in small gardens. It was originally planted as the stock of some rose variety. This is one of the reasons why the briar is to be preferred as a rose stock, for it does not sucker so freely. Other subjects which may give similar trouble are apples, pears, cherries, plums, peaches, nectarines, variegated, weeping or other special forms of ornamental trees and conifers, azaleas, rhododendrons, lilacs, brooms and hollies. Where a choice is offered by the nurseryman between grafted plants and those on their own roots, it is almost always wiser to choose the latter. There is no excuse for budding and grafting in instances where layering is equally successful, for besides the nuisance of suckers the plants are sometimes less healthy, especially lilacs, conifers and rhododendrons. The exception is supplied in brooms, which are always more satisfactory when worked upon laburnum stocks.

In this chapter I have endeavoured to cover a wide field. There has been little attempt to describe how actual operations are carried out, but rather to give a general impression as to the useful services which are attendant upon considerate pruning. Where actual operations have been mentioned, no attempt has been made to give complete directions, which will be dealt with in subsequent chapters. This is because I have thought it wisest to give a more or less theoretical outline of the benefits before going on to the practical consideration of the subject.

CHAPTER TWO

SPECIALISED FORMS OF PRUNING

THERE are five methods of specialised pruning which will be referred to from time to time in following chapters. They are: Root Pruning, Ringing, Spur Pruning, Summer Pruning and Peach Pruning. All five processes are important, and each must be dealt with in detail. Those who are anxious to understand the principles which govern the application of pruning will be repaid for studying this chapter before going on to the practical side of the question which is dealt with in the latter part of the book. Most of these methods are to be considered, in the main, in connection with the treatment of all types of fruit trees, but they may be extended to other fields, especially flowering shrubs and trees.

Root Pruning.—The conditions which necessitate the application of root pruning have already, in some measure, been dealt with. It must be carried out when there is an uneven balance between the growth of root and stem to such an extent that the subject makes too much growth and consequently produces little or no flower and fruit. The condition is described as being uneven, because although there is a direct balance between the amount of root and top growth made, in such cases as those under consideration the rooting system has run amok, and must be restrained in order that there may be a corresponding slackening off in the vigour of top growth. The tree will then settle down to an even rate of growth and will commence to flower and fruit.

Root pruning is often necessary in young trees, and sometimes in older ones, and is frequently practised on apples, pears, plums, cherries, peaches, nectarines, apricots, figs, grape vines, as well as ornamental trees and shrubs. The most likely subjects are apples, pears, plums and cherries when grown as trained trees, the first two as cordons and espaliers, and the last-named as fan-trained trees. These varieties of fruit may be purchased as grafted specimens on root stocks of varying vigour. That is to say, the nurseryman selects a definite type of stock, not only for the type of tree to be trained, but also bearing in mind the individual vigour of the variety being grafted. This is not really a subject to be discussed in detail in this book, but it is mentioned because it is unfortunately sometimes the case that trees are sold as cordons or fan trained, which should have been grafted on weak rooting stocks, but instead free growing stocks have been used. This might work out satisfactorily on very poor soils, but in rich ground is certain to result in growth which may call for repeated root pruning. Tap roots which have grown strongly into the subsoil—where they find an abundance of moisture—are the cause of the trouble, and they must be severed close to the stem of the tree. Strong roots are also frequently found close to the soil surface, and where there is need for drastic root pruning they must also be shortened back. It is important to make every cut as cleanly as possible. Jagged cuts or tears result in rotting, whereas clean cuts often lead to the production of fibrous roots.

Young trees which have been planted up to five or six years are best lifted completely from the ground when requiring root pruning. Strong roots can then be cut back and the tree firmly replanted. It is wise to take the precaution of staking replanted trees to keep them from being blown over. Incidentally, when staking a tree, it is always wise, first to drive in the stake, and then to plant the tree up to it. If the reverse is done, roots are frequently damaged by the point of the stake as it is being driven down. Larger trees which require root pruning must receive different treatment. A semi-circular trench must be taken out at a radius from the trunk of from 3 feet upwards, according to the size of the specimen. This must be dug out to a depth of 3 or 4 feet, and all strong growing roots must be severed. The digging should also be continued inwards from the bottom of the trench, in order to intercept those roots which have grown downwards. It is generally here that the worst offending tap roots are to be found. The soil can then be replaced, and if in the following season the tree is still found to be too vigorous, the remaining half circumference can be treated in the same manner. It is unwise to dig entirely round in one operation, as the removal of so many of the tree's principal anchors may result in its being blown over during severe storms.

It is most important that when soil is being put back following this operation that it should be thoroughly firm. Fill in the trench methodically layer by layer, using a rammer. Firm ground encourages the production of fibrous roots.

Wall-trained Trees.—Trees planted against walls, such as fan-trained peaches and plums, frequently need root pruning, especially in the earlier stages of growth, but this is rather a matter for discussion under the heading of cultivation, for such trees should have their root run restricted both in depth and in area. When the latter precaution has not been taken and the trees require it, root pruning may be carried out as suggested for other trees.

The same remarks apply to figs, but here again root pruning should not be necessary with proper cultivation. This fruit should always be planted in the poorest possible soil in order to restrict growth and encourage bearing.

Where peaches, nectarines and vines are grown in borders under glass they should have a restricted root run, which should always be confined to the borders in the houses, and never to the borders in the open, which are not under the proper control of the cultivator. Root pruning is sometimes necessary even when rooting is entirely within the house, especially with young peaches and nectarines. Where roots are allowed to grow into an outside border as well, an endeavour should be made gradually to dispense with those outside by cutting away the strongest first, and eventually every root. The inside border may then be bricked up so as to prevent further root action outside.

Time of Operation.—Whilst I have never heard of it having been done on a large scale, it is possible in extreme cases to root prune during the growing season. The best months are October and November and again in March and April. Never tackle the job if the ground is wet, and remember that it is real hard work. See that the spade is well sharpened. If the tree is a large one a mattock will be needed.

A great deal has been written about root pruning at various times. Those who have actually done the work will agree that it is satisfactory on smaller trees, but on very large ones I prefer ringing, a process which was mentioned in Chapter One. It has the same effect as root pruning and is simpler in accomplishment.

Transplanting Large Trees.—Before dealing with ringing in more detail I should like to mention one more point which is connected, in a way, with root pruning, although it has not so much to do with pruning. It concerns the proposed transplanting of large specimens of any kind. Where it is decided to move a large tree, it is wise to carry out an operation which is tantamount to root pruning, twelve months before the moving. Encircle the tree as before with a trench, cutting all strong roots. Make this trench as close as you dare to the main stem. A little exploration is better than the following of printed dimensions. Having rammed the soil thoroughly, and providing the tree with support if considered necessary, leave the tree for a year, and then carefully lift, taking care to preserve the fibrous roots which will have formed in the area where the first trench was dug, together with the soil adhering. September and October would be the best months for both operations.

Ringing.—It would be wise to make clear at the outset that this form of pruning is not recommended for stone fruits. It is primarily for apples and pears, and for other types of trees or even large shrubs, where curtailment in vigour is desired. From the brief outline already given of this operation, it will be seen that it would be a simple matter to vary the effect of ringing by slightly lengthening or shortening the two semicircles of bark removed (see Chapter One). That is to say, the two channels cut in the tree would either overlap or not quite meet an imaginary vertical line between them. The former is the more drastic, but for most purposes the precise semicircle on either side is sufficiently effective on very vigorous trees.

Each channel should be from $\frac{1}{2}$ to $\frac{3}{4}$ inch in width, and the two should be separated by about 6 inches of trunk. The best time for the operation is just before, or whilst, the trees are in flower. I treated fifty trees of apple (D'Arcy Spice) on 7th May 1944. These are fifteen-year-old trees which have scarcely ever produced a flower, let alone anything of a crop, despite consistent light pruning. I am glad to say that at the time of writing (January 1945) they are well covered with fruit bud. It would appear, on the face of it, an unkind period of the growth of the tree during which to make a severe surgical operation, but it is at this time that the flow of sap is most active and the healing of the cuts most rapid.

I do not think it matters much as to which portion of the main trunk is selected for making the cuts. From the point of view of easiness in operation, the higher the better on trees which have only a short leg. An examination of most trunks, however, will be a guide in itself, because the job is more easily accomplished where the bark is smooth and there is an absence of knots, swellings or healed wounds where low limbs have previously been removed.

For carrying out the work a very sharp pruning knife with a first-class point is an essential. Some people like to have a half-inch chisel handy. Personally, I have not found it necessary. Remember, too, that a dry sack is wanted for the operator to lie upon if the cut is to be made low down, or a box to sit on for higher work. A certain amount of force has got to be exerted with a keen edge in use, and the greater the comfort, the less likelihood of an accident.

If the actual operation has not been attempted previously, I think the wisest first step is to mark out the cuts on the trunk. A piece of cardboard can be folded round the trunk to act as a ruler and the line marked thinly with a pointed chalk or coloured pencil, having regard to the dimensions already given. Now for the most difficult part of the task. The depth to which the cut is made is all important. It must penetrate through the bark and the soft tissues beneath it until hard wood is reached. This obviously varies with the size of the tree, but it is not likely to be less than $\frac{1}{8}$ inch or much more than $\frac{1}{4}$ inch, unless the tree is exceptionally large. Holding the knife in the right hand, and starting at the left end of one of the semi-circles, draw the knife slowly along each line, pressing the point well home with the fingers of the left hand. It may be necessary to run the knife once or twice more along each line, but it is generally quite evident when firm wood has been reached. Finally make the short incision at each end, and a similar one somewhere nearly half-way between them. Starting from this central cut, lever out the rind which is to be removed in either direction with the point of the knife. If the cuts have been made to the correct depth, and the work is being done at the correct time, the strips should now peel out without any difficulty. Trim up the cuts if there are any thin splinters left attached to the bark, and then either paint the wound with undiluted tar oil or Stockholm tar, or better still, if available, cover with adhesive tape.

A certain amount of patience, and a great amount of care, is necessary in carrying out this work for the first time. Remember that if you wish to bring an overvigorous tree into bearing, and assuming that very light pruning has failed to accomplish this, the only alternative to ringing is root pruning. Confronted with a large tree, I should have no hesitation which method to adopt. To ring a tree might at the outside take half an hour, whilst root pruning a large tree might well take up the best part of a day. The methods are equally effective.

Spur Pruning.—In the preceding two forms of specialised pruning I have dealt with operations which may be carried out upon a variety of subjects. In all instances, however, the methods employed would be similar. It has therefore been possible to describe them both in theory and practice, giving details as to how the work should be done.

Spur pruning is a term which embraces varying methods, and is regularly employed on a large number of different subjects, mostly certain types of fruit such as apples, pears, plums and sweet cherries (the last two as fan-trained trees), gooseberries, red and white currants, filbert and hazel nuts, besides many flowering shrubs and climbers. Because the process varies so much in its method of application I can at this stage deal with the matter in theory only. In later chapters more elaborate details will be given with each subject requiring spur pruning. The whole question is one of great importance and has given rise to much discussion, experiment and revision of ideas, and it is necessary fully to understand the theory of it before passing on to the practical. I shall endeavour to be as lucid as possible, but the reader will appreciate the difficulty of describing the subject for treatment at the same time as the method employed.

Spur pruning, or 'spurring', embodies the treatment applied during the dormant period to one-year-old wood which has been produced as side shoots from main branches throughout

Above: Well-spurred apples trained on the oblique single-stemmed cordon system.

Right: The method of filling in the end of a row of oblique trained cordon fruit trees

Fruit buds formed at the tips of side shoots on Apple Worcester Pearmain.

The result of dehorning an apple tree. Note strong growth on upper half.

The result of correct spur pruning of a red currant (left) compared with wrong treatment resulting in much strong but unfruitful growth (right). Note the open centre of the correctly pruned bush.

Stages in the pruning of a gooseberry to correct a weeping habit. Cuts on the leading shoots retained are to a bud facing upwards.

Below : A typical peach growth in spring before disbudding commences.

Above : The same growth after some disbudding has been done. Still more shoots will be removed in the middle region.

their length. It controls the position and regulates the quantity of fruiting wood into which these side shoots shall be transformed. It is practised on subjects which fruit on two-year-old wood or older, and the process is assisted in some cases, but not in all, by a shortening of the young wood in question during the previous summer (summer pruning).

Having attempted a definition, it now remains to study the subject from the beginning. It will first be necessary to study parts of a tree in order that the various types of growth and buds described may be readily identified and recognised. For purposes of demonstration, consider a single branch of apple or pear, and take first of all the different types of bud which it shows.

(*a*) **Growth Buds.**—Whenever demonstrating pruning I always mention first of all the fact that in my humble opinion this class of bud has been given an unfortunate name. I wish to emphasise the fact that the sole purpose and function of these buds is not, as the name implies, to produce growth. They have another and more important purpose. However, I will describe them first and then go on to explain their characteristics.

There is no difficulty in distinguishing growth buds, for they are produced in great numbers on young wood. Examined during the winter on one-year-old wood, they will be seen to be pointed and lying flat throughout the whole length of each shoot. Now if all these buds produced shoots I would have no quarrel with the generally accepted name. But they do not. A large number of them are converted into fruit buds during their second year of existence, whilst a third, and much smaller proportion, remain dormant. If I have succeeded in making my point clear, I shall have rendered the reader great service, because, since growth buds are borne on young wood and are readily and naturally converted into fruit buds, this young wood is a potential of fruit production and must not be submitted to the annual beheading which is so frequently the case. The proportion in which growth buds produce shoots, fruit buds, or remain dormant, depends upon the subject, its vigour and the manner of pruning, and will be dealt with fully in subsequent discussion.

(*b*) **Flower Buds.**—This class of bud, equally well termed

C

cutting occurred the position is unfortunate. No fruit bud has formed and there are more shoots than ever before. It is surprising how many people indulge in this process of annual hard cutting. It is in all sense of the word a fruitless pursuit and must be discouraged.

I have made no mention of treatment of young shoots from existing fruit spurs. It is only in the rare event of such a shoot being required to form the foundation of a new branch that it would be left at almost full length. If it is desired to increase the size of the spur use the medium treatment; but in cases where the spur is already well formed, severe cutting or entire removal is obviously permissible.

I have discussed this subject in theory now at some length and the reader may well be getting tired of so much detail. The important facts are that it is possible to make short fruit spurs if you want them, but it is also possible, by the judicious retention of young wood, vastly to increase the fruiting capabilities of most trees. How this is accomplished will be dealt with in detail under the headings of each subject requiring such treatment, so that there, for the moment, the subject may be left.

Summer Pruning.—There has been much controversy during recent years as to the advantages and disadvantages which accrue from the process known as summer pruning. In some cases it is advantageous that the shortening back of lateral growths should be done during the summer months instead of after the fall of the leaves, as is general with most pruning done in the orchard. The advantage of summer pruning is that it enables the operator to curtail growth of laterals, removing a certain amount of leafy growth which otherwise would shade the existing fruits which are borne on the main branch. Sunshine is essential to the formation of the highest-class fruit, and without it high colouring of well-sized fruits cannot be expected. I grow a large number of Cox's Orange commercially, some on cordons and some on bush trees. All trees receive the same spraying programme, and manuring to the best of my ability is done as required. The cordons are summer pruned always, but the bush trees are not. The fruit from the former is always better in finish and keeps a little better too. Whilst I doubt if there is any difference in the flavour, there is no doubt as to which trees to visit for show specimens.

When summer pruning for the benefit of fruit, remember that the removal of leaves necessitates the loss of a certain amount of the plant's food-manufacturing process. Consequently, whilst fruit is swelling and developing, it is desirable that every possible leaf should be allowed to remain, and it is

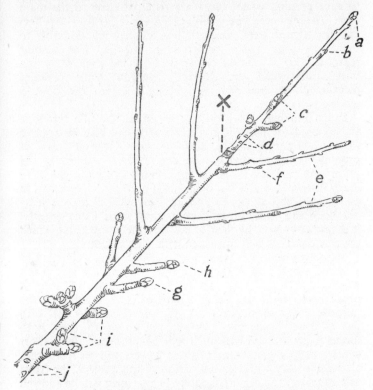

TYPICAL TWO-YEAR-OLD APPLE SHOOT.

a, Tip bud ; *b*, growth bud ; *c*, fruit buds ; *d*, poorly developed growth buds ; *e*, laterals produced from strong growth buds ; *f*, mixed bud that may develop into fruit bud if shoot is correctly pruned ; *g*, short laterals produced by mixed buds ; *h*, fruit bud at tip of lateral ; *i*, spurs ; *j*, dormant buds ; *x*, juncture between one-year and two-year-old wood.

CHAPTER THREE

PRUNING AT PLANTING TIME

It is unwise to carry out any other than essential pruning at the actual time of planting. The reason for this is that the transplanting in itself is a check, especially if the subjects have been for some time in transit from the nursery. Certain things which are more or less obvious must be done, and will not in any way increase the hazards of transplanting. What I should describe as essential would only consist of careful removal of any broken shoots, together with a shortening back of damaged roots of any kind, and also of any strong tap roots.

In cases where further pruning is essential during the same season as planting, leave as great a length of time as possible between the two operations, but do not delay until after growth has started. Late planted shrubs and fruit trees are generally also a bit late in starting into growth, which will give a respite of a week or so. But it should always be remembered that pruning is in itself a check, quite apart from the stimulating influence it eventually has, and should not be done at planting time.

There are certain subjects which must receive drastic treatment in the way of pruning during the winter or early spring after planting. I know it seems a little unkind to suggest that having purchased a bush, prepared the ground and planted it, that a few weeks later it must be cut down to ground level. For subjects which need it, however, this is sound advice and in fact essential if success is to follow.

Any varieties of fruit which bear on one-year-old wood must be treated in this way. They are sent out from nurseries well furnished with young wood, which if left unpruned, must perforce carry out the function of flower and fruit production. Such bearing is bound to absorb far more energy than a freshly planted tree can spare, with the unavoidable result that no new young wood is made, and there is consequently no provision for next year's crop. It is obviously far more satisfactory to sacrifice a meagre supply of first year's fruit and to establish a vigorous young bush which will bear generously the second and subsequent years. These instructions for hard pruning of freshly planted fruits applies to black currants, raspberries, loganberries and all types of black-berries. With red and white currants and gooseberries, if you are being wise and are buying young two-year-olds, treat them with equal severity. With older bushes of these three fruits, cut to within a bud or two of the base of the young wood only.

The Lloyd George variety of raspberry cannot be prevented from fruiting the first year after planting, because it has a habit of producing blossoms at the end of current season's wood, in the same manner as the true autumn fruiting rasp-berry. I do not think this matters in the least, providing the canes are making good growth, and the fruit will be doubly welcome, appearing as it does so late in the season, and always being of exceptional quality.

Certain flowering shrubs which produce their blossoms on one-year-old wood should be well pruned soon after planting, although it need not be quite so drastic a treatment as that suggested for the fruits listed above. I would certainly cut out all weak shoots and reduce the number of the potential blossom-bearing ones. The following require such treatment: *Buddleia alternifolia*, deutzias, diervillas, exochordas, forsythias, *Hypericum patulum* and varieties, kerrias, philadelphus, loniceras (the deciduous shrubby species only, such as *Standishii tartarica* and *thibetica*), ribes, *Spiræas arguta*, *S. canescens*, *S. prunifolia*, *S. Reevesiana*, *S. Thunberghii*, *S. Van Houttei* and *S. Veitchii*, and finally symphoricarpus.

This is the first list of shrubs given. It will be noticed that some kinds are mentioned in the plural, which infers that all species and varieties are included, others in the singular, which means that there is only one species in general cultivation. Where one or more species are mentioned it infers that there are others in the same genus requiring different treatment. For example, selecting from the list at random, it will be seen that deutzias are mentioned. It is intended that the reader should gather that all deutzias require similar handling on the lines suggested. On the other hand, *Buddleia alternifolia* is mentioned as a species, showing that there are other kinds obtaining fruit in the first year is not to be recommended, and a pound of fruit taken in the first year may well result in the necessity of cutting the tree so hard that it is reduced to the size of a much younger one and not a very happy specimen at that. My advice to intending planters is to start with young stock, maidens if you like, and if you follow the instructions of a later chapter you will very quickly build a strong tree which will soon be giving generous crops. I say all this in a book on pruning because, firstly, a sound and strong tree must be the only thought before there can be fruit; and secondly, because it is very difficult successfully to build up a satisfactory tree that has been moved as a four- or five-year-old and crippled by excessive early bearing. It is even more difficult to give pruning instructions as to how to make the attempt.

Other Fruits.—The remaining fruits will not require any pruning in the dormant stage following planting, save the young grape vine, which must be shortened back to about 5 feet. Whilst it does not strictly relate to the dormant period, mention should also be made of young strawberries planted after September. They should not be allowed to fruit in their first season, and the blossoms should be removed as soon as they appear during May.

CHAPTER FOUR

PRUNING IN PRACTICE

Knife *v*. Sécateurs.—The next point to consider is how the actual operation of pruning is carried out. Until a few years back the most experienced gardeners and nurserymen would use no other tool than the knife, which had always been recognised as the only really satisfactory way. It is absolutely essential that every cut that is made should be quite clean, so that loss of sap is reduced to a minimum and healing is brought about as quickly as possible. The latter is indirectly important from the point of view of exclusion of fungus diseases. Within the last few years, however, a perfected form of sécateurs has been put on the market. The old-fashioned type merely produced a jagged cut, which always resulted in bruising the wood, but the Rolcut sécateurs have in a large degree obviated this fault. This tool, with a blade of the finest tempered steel on one side and a metal anvil on the other, has a slight drawing action of the blade as it cuts. Consequently, with a little practice it is possible always to make clean cuts on wood which is not more than about $\frac{3}{8}$ inch in thickness. (This is a little thicker than a lead pencil.) The large size of Rolcut sécateur will cut wood up to $\frac{3}{4}$ inch in thickness, but it may slightly bruise the bark in so doing, a defect which is quickly remedied with a knife. This tool has now so thoroughly established itself that it is used in many first-class nurseries and commercial orchards where the old-fashioned type of sécateur was not permitted.

Sécateurs are more simple and quicker to use than the knife, and it is possible for a child to use them quite safely and without much effort.

Many gardeners, however, still prefer to make use of a high-class pruning knife, and there is certainly a great deal of satisfaction to be obtained from its proper use. The cuts are always neat and clean when properly done, but there is always the danger that the blade will travel further than was intended, and either damage the tree or the operator. Pruning hand so as to steady it. Place the sécateurs in the most convenient way to make the cut, but the anvil or non-cutting side must not touch the bud. The safest way to make the cut is for the knife edge of the sécateur blade to start immediately above the bud and on the same side, and to cut through the shoot to the opposite side. Reasoning this out, it will be seen that the easiest position for the pruner to stand is with the bud pointing either straight towards him, or towards his left. Conversely the most difficult are those pointing to the right or those on the other side of the shoot which points away, the former because if you put the tool naturally to the shoot, the anvil will be right on the bud, and if the cut is made the bud will be bruised, and the latter because it cannot be properly seen. If there is no visible bud conveniently placed at the point where you consider the cut ought to be made, then shift your position so that you are enabled to do so.

In making the cut, take great care not to turn the wrist, or, in other words, avoid a wrenching movement. Sécateurs are not to be used like wire cutters. Keep your eye on the bud until the cut is made. There is a great temptation when a little efficiency is attained and work has to be done quickly to look around for the next cut before the one in hand is made, and bad results are bound to follow. Remember the golfer's golden rule, and watch each cut until it is made.

When cutting shoots which are much over half an inch in thickness it may be necessary to use both hands, the base of each palm being used to press the handles. To cut such shoots, remember that greatest leverage is obtained near the apex of blade and anvil, so open the sécateurs as wide as you can and push them gently forwards towards the shoot before cutting. If you get stuck half-way, don't wrench and tussle, but remove the sécateurs and start again. You will find that the second application to the same cut enables the jaws to get a little further in and the cut is easily finished. In all such cases cutting is simplified if a slight pressure downwards is made on the branch to be removed, but this should not be applied until the blade is half-way through.

Wherever bark is slightly torn by the anvil of sécateurs, the knife ought to be used to trim the wound. If the instructions

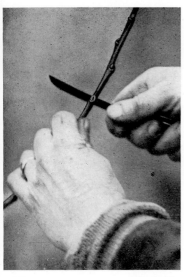

The correct way to prune with a knife.
The shoot is held firmly just below the
point at which it is to be cut.

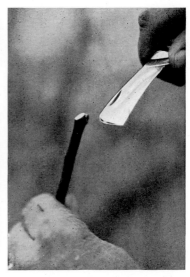

The finish of the knife cut. Note
that the blade has come out just above
a bud.

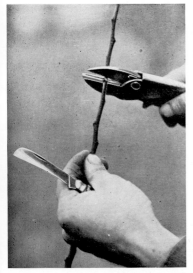

The correct method of pruning with
sécateurs, the blade square to, and
immediately above, a bud.

Smoothing the surface of a large cut
made with a saw. This will afterwards
be painted over to assist healing.

Pruning leaders of bush apple trees. Note the triangular 'steps', which do not touch the branches.

A possible 'replacement leader'. The shoot represents two years' growth and the lower part was tipped the previous winter.

Another apple shoot which was lightly tipped the previous winter. In this case it is being shortened to a fruit bud to form a fruiting lateral.

given have been followed out the damage will only be slight, and will be on the side opposite the bud. One stroke of the knife should be sufficient. It should be drawn from just below the torn bark on the damaged side towards the bud, and at such an angle that by the time the bud is reached no wood is emoved. If the original sécateur cut was square, the second cut will be found to be only slightly sloping. All this may sound a great deal, but in actual operation the whole thing should not take more than two seconds. There are right and wrong ways of doing most jobs, and the right one is the quickest and most satisfactory in the long run. I have to do a lot of pruning in winter time and find that the work may extend to four months. My practice is invariably to carry a knife in the left hand, whilst sécateurs are used in the right. If a rectifying knife cut has to be made, it takes but little time for the two tools to change hands for the operation and back again, although with practice I have found it possible to make all but the most difficult knife cuts with the left hand.

Mention has been made of securing the shoot to be pruned with the left hand. This can easily be done with the thumb and forefinger whilst the rest of the hand holds the knife. It is not necessary to hold every shoot, although the beginner is advised to do so. A little experience will soon show when this added precaution is necessary. Never hold the shoot above the point to be severed, always below.

The Knife.—Before starting to use a knife, see that it is really sharp. If you are not skilled in the operation of sharpening, get a carpenter or ironmonger to show you how it is done, and remember that an oilstone is an essential, because a knife in constant use needs touching up two or three times a day. When cutting an ordinary shoot to a bud, the knife should come through the shoot in one easy pull. The bud must point to the operator as before, but the cut starts on the side behind the bud, the knife travelling towards the pruner. The left hand must invariably be used to steady the shoot at a point about 2 inches below the cut. For this type of cut the right-hand thumb is best folded comfortably out of harm's way over the forefinger, incidentally assisting in holding the knife securely.

D

the best results. With this class, which are mostly deciduous kinds which flower either on wood of the current season or on last year's wood, it is only right to mention that, left to their own devices, they will continue to flower for quite a few seasons, and flower well. But if no pruning is done vigour and blossoms gradually deteriorate, and, what is worse, there is a gradual increase in height which is made at the expense of bare and useless old wood at the base. Correct pruning, which is in all cases perfectly simple, retains healthy vigour, a free flowering habit of natural appearance, and ensures freedom from a gaunt and drawn-up picture by eliminating an accumulation of bare wood which would otherwise be built up in the lower part of the shrub.

It will be seen, therefore, that it is necessary to consider several types of shrubs in order to deal with the subject of pruning in a comprehensive manner. It is an important matter, but none the less quite readily understood even by those who have little gardening experience.

Evergreens.—I have already mentioned that there are a number of shrubs which require little or no pruning. The majority of this section is composed of evergreens, which, almost without exception, will be quite happy with no pruning at all. It sometimes becomes necessary, however, to restrict them within bounds, and a safe rule to follow is to cut them back in late spring, when all danger of frost is over.

In the case of magnolia (evergreen species), myrica and olearia, when cutting back is necessary each branch dealt with should be cut entirely and cleanly away from the base, leaving no short stumps.

Many other kinds need not be treated in such a drastic manner, but may be cut back to a dormant bud, when they will break into growth. Those which flower comparatively early in the year may, if desired, be left until their blossoms have faded; but it must be borne in mind that the later they are pruned the less chance there will be of formation of wood for next year's flowering. Shrubs to which these remarks apply include hollies in variety, aucubas, choisya, cotoneaster, euonymus, osmanthus, phillyræa, rhododendrons, berberis, ulex (gorse), coronilla, abelias, andromedas, azara, buddleia, ceanothus, cistus, escallonias, *Garrya elliptica*, leptospermums, *Phlomis fruticosa*, pyracanthas, *Senecio Grayii* and viburnums. It should be noted that evergreen species only of the foregoing families are indicated; several of the subjects embrace deciduous species also, but these require different treatment.

Some evergreens are subject to damage, which may be quite serious, by late spring frosts. I have sometimes seen rhododendrons cruelly treated in this way at a time when they have been in full flower. They present a most pitiful spectacle when this happens, the blossoms, young leaves and shoots turning quite black, and the whole shrub looking for all the world as though it were dead. Many other shrubs which, like the rhododendron, may be quite hardy through the winter whilst they are not growing, are susceptible to damage when they have started into growth. Such kinds as escallonias, olearias and cistus are examples. Other shrubs which are less hardy may be damaged in winter either by frost or, more likely still, by continued, drying, icy winds in the early part of the year.

Whenever serious damage is caused either by winter or spring conditions, carry on in the same way as advised for restricting growth; that is to say, wait for the end of May or first week in June, and then cut back to sound wood. It is surprising how often an evergreen which looks practically dead will respond to this treatment. It may not always be possible to find a bud, either dormant or prominent, as though wishing to grow. This will not matter, as growth will start if you have cut to sound wood, although it is possible that a snag of dead wood may be found later which should be removed.

In cutting evergreen shrubs which are healthy with a view to restricting or even reducing in size, endeavour to remove entire shoots or even small branches, rather than shorten them back. When doing this particular job I like to leave the specimen looking as though it had not been pruned at all, except that it is smaller; that is to say, the individuality of growth is retained. This is not so hard to accomplish as it may sound. Where there is serious damage, however, it is impossible to hide the fact that the pruner has been at work. Following a really severe frost, it may be necessary to remove quite a lot of wood before sound growth is reached, and it is fortunate that these circumstances are comparatively rare.

Among the evergreens, rhododendrons and andromedas should not be allowed to set seed, and blossoms should be removed together with those of azaleas (which are mostly deciduous but generally grown in the same company) as soon as they are faded. This may sound trivial, but is important, as these plants set heavy crops of seed which, if allowed to mature, may jeopardise next year's flowers. It is a practice regularly carried out in all nurseries where these plants are grown. Magnolias, too, sometimes set seed, and I think it a wise plan to prevent this on young trees.

The dwarf-growing heaths are best lightly trimmed over with shears after flowering whenever it is found necessary to restrict their growth in the rock garden or when used for edging purposes. In the heath garden they may be allowed to grow naturally except possibly on the outsides of plantations, where it is advisable to keep them bushy, so preventing any possibility of a straggling appearance. Tree heaths should not be touched.

There are a few choice and rather rare evergreens, whose natural mode of growth and appearance is perhaps better described as bare stemmed rather than leggy. Those which I have in mind, such as arbutus, *Berberis japonica* and varieties *hyemalis* and *Bealii*, pieris, photinias and some of the rarer rhododendron species, should, of course, never be cut unless they are damaged. If they are considered too gaunt in appearance, the remedy here is to plant something beneath them, but never to shorten the stems.

Deciduous Shrubs.—There are quite a number of deciduous shrubs which normally require no pruning; that is to say, they will flower at their best if left to continue undisturbed. Removal of suckers, or broken shoots, must, of course, receive attention. Some of these kinds, especially those which will eventually make small trees, such as flowering cherries or ornamental crabs, may require some attention to thinning and training during the first year or two, but this amounts to very little on well-grown nursery stock. It is important to see that none of the young branches cross or are likely to rub against each other.

Classified Shrub Pruning

So far I have dealt with shrubs which, under ordinary conditions, require no attention to pruning in the sense of hard cutting of wood. It is now necessary to pass on to the various types which will require one of several different methods of pruning. Before doing so, mention must be made of the Classified Shrub Pruning List which will be found at the end of the chapter. This consists of a reasonably comprehensive list of shrubs arranged alphabetically. In making this list I have tried to include all those shrubs which are likely to be found in most amateurs' gardens. Against each will be found letters and numerals denoting treatment required and time of operation. For quick reference, a key gives the meaning of the letters and numerals, but for those who require more detailed information, the following notes will show the different types of pruning, together with the selected key letter which refers to each method. For example, those shrubs which have been already mentioned, which require no pruning, have the letter A. I am obliged to include these in the list, because, although it is reasonably complete, there may be omissions of some of the rarer kinds. If the list included only varieties requiring pruning, it might be assumed that a shrub not listed did not require pruning, which might be inaccurate. In any case, I feel that it is reassuring to find a comprehensive list which is most likely to include the majority of shrubs found in all but collectors' gardens. At the same time the necessity of including lists whilst describing the different methods of pruning is avoided. The reader has merely to note the letter referring to each method, and then turn to the Classified List. The numbers 1 to 12 refer to the calendar months.

Deciduous Shrubs Flowering on Current Season's Wood (denoted in Key by B).—This class of shrub, which is extensive, is very simply dealt with at pruning time. In order that there may be no mistake about their method of growth and flowering, they may be likened to herbaceous plants in that they make growth and flower upon it in the same season. Here is a class of plants where strong growth is desirable to obtain the best results. Supposing at the end of the first year's growth they are left unpruned. The shoots, being woody, will not die back entirely as is the case with herbaceous plants, but will persist through the winter. Left undisturbed, these shoots, which are well covered with growth buds, would produce a thicket of weak straggling shoots the following year. The pruner should aim at getting a few strong shoots only, and this is readily done by cutting all young growth down to the ground level or just above it, and by thinning the resultant young shoots if necessary.

There are four slight variations in this class of shrub.

(1) The type described, which are perfectly hardy and may be pruned hard back in the winter (B, 12, 1, 2).

(2) Are similar to type (1) but their young shoots are liable to frost damage if encouraged into premature growth, and pruning is best delayed until April (B, 4).

(3) A class embodying both types (1) and (2) in which it is possible, if desired, gradually to build up a framework of old wood and thus increase the height and size of the specimen. This would be accomplished by pruning hard the first year to obtain strong growth. Three of these shoots would be retained at about half length during the second pruning, young shoots from the ground level and from the lower parts of the selected shoots being removed. This process would be continued until the required size was obtained, and thereafter pruning would consist of removing all the young wood of the previous season save for a few buds at the base of each. If at any time it was desired to reduce the size there would be no harm done in cutting hard back into old wood. A typical example of this type is the purple buddleia, and I have frequently taken the saw to this shrub where it was overgrown and cut it down to the ground (B (a)).

(4) Represents a small class of shrubs of type (1) which are grown partly for the bright colouring of their stems. These exhibit their beauty through the winter months, and for this reason, although they are perfectly hardy, pruning is delayed until spring (B, 3, 4).

Shrubs Flowering on One-Year-Old Wood.—The next type for consideration are those shrubs which flower from wood made during the previous summer. The aim here must be to retain one-year-old shoots which have not as yet produced their blossom, and at the same time to encourage the formation of young shoots for next year's flowering. It must be appreciated that once flowering is over, the wood which has produced the blossoms is useless except for the production of next year's wood, which may be seen at the earliest stage of its formation in the form of young shoots, which are produced either previously to, or concurrently with, the blossoms; that is to say, that any one-year-old shoot produces both flowers and shoots, and two-year-old wood is undesirable.

In order to understand the pruning of these they must be divided into two classes.

(1) Those which flower early in the year (C). Here the pruning consists of cutting back, immediately after flowering, all wood which produced flowers, making the cut as low down as possible consistent with retaining one or two young shoots at the base. Thus, the old flowering wood which is now useless is removed, and at the same time the young shoots retained have the rest of the growing season before them, during which time they will develop into strong shoots for next year's flowering.

(2) Those which flower later in the year (D) and (E). In this case, matters are a little more complicated owing to the fact that numerous young shoots are produced throughout the length of the flowering wood. It is impossible to prune early in the year, because this would result in the cutting away of the season's flowers. On the other hand, if no pruning at all is done during the growing season, it is probable that too many young shoots will be produced for next year's flowering. One or two strong growths are better than half a dozen or more weaker ones. It is the problem of peach pruning (see Chapter Two) all over again, and there is no doubt that in order to get the best from this class of shrub it is wise to restrict the number of young side shoots produced from the flowering wood, and to retain about two only. Those retained should be selected from as near the base of the one-year-old wood as possible, so that when the time comes for the cutting out of the then useless flowering wood by pruning to the topmost of the retained young shoots, there will be little of the original shoot left on the specimen. The selection of these two young basal shoots will take place during the growing

Ornamental Trees.—Those which are planted with the intention of providing large specimens are generally left to take care of themselves after they have been given their final position in the garden. If no pruning at all is done to these trees they may become lopsided in shape, and a little attention in the early stages may prevent this. It may safely be said that the earlier any necessary work is done, the less will be the attention required at a later period. A great deal can be done by pinching strong side shoots which at any time appear to challenge the leading shoot. In many cases it is advisable to secure the latter with a bamboo cane, which may be fastened lower down on the main trunk. This is particularly necessary with most conifers, because if once the leader is damaged it becomes rather difficult to replace. In the event of an accident to a leader in this class of tree the only procedure is to cut back to the nearest whorl of small branches. Several new growths will appear, and the strongest of these must be selected and the remainder pinched out.

With many of the ornamental crabs and cherries much can be accomplished in the early stages by means of selecting the strongest shoots and encouraging them to grow in the desired directions by tying a thin cane to support one or more of them. Thus one may prevent young branches from crossing or overcrowding. This work is rather important, because so many of this type of trees are liable to bleed badly if branches are removed at a later date.

Large growing trees, such as chestnuts, limes and elms, should be encouraged to form a pyramidal shape as far as possible. By this means a secure structure is built up, and there is little danger of limbs becoming blown off when the tree is fully grown.

Removal of Large Limbs.—When it is found necessary to sacrifice entire branches either through damage or disease a certain amount of care is necessary. It is generally accepted that November is the best time of the year for this class of work. The golden rule to bear in mind is to remove small pieces at a time, whilst the last piece of all should be extremely light in weight. This is the only way of being certain of making a clean cut. The last cut should be made as close to the main trunk as possible. Never leave a stump projecting. This will most probably die back to the main trunk, affording a means of ready access for fungus diseases. All cuts should be painted over with coal tar or Stockholm tar, and such applications repeated if they have worn off before the cut has healed over completely.

Treatment of Overgrown Borders.—I think that the improvement of overgrown shrub borders is fascinating work, because with a little ingenuity a great deal can be accomplished. After any undesirables have been grubbed out the remainder can generally be dealt with quite easily and satisfactorily if a little care is exercised.

I have explained how evergreen subjects may be severely reduced in size without ill effect. With overgrown deciduous subjects, it is necessary first of all to recognise on what type of wood flower is produced. This will be simply accomplished, either by observation or by getting each subject named correctly, and referring to the Key at the end of the chapter to discover into which class it falls. Having done this, it will be found that quite a number will be listed in category B, which means that they may be safely cut back very hard either to old wood or to the ground. Those listed under C may be drastically thinned during winter. It may not be possible to leave any young wood near the base in doing this, but the hard cutting will, in itself, encourage fresh growth to spring from the ground, and the following winter pruning will be simple.

Any deciduous shrubs remaining, falling in category A and therefore requiring no pruning under normal conditions, may require careful handling, as many of them are very choice. Many of them are fortunately not of very vigorous constitution and may not require reducing in size (I am thinking of deciduous magnolias, the Judas tree, the flowering quinces, sometimes called japonicas, the witch hazels and the flowering cornels.

Where it is found absolutely necessary to cut them the safest plan would be to remove entire branches rather than to adopt a systematic shortening back, and the best time for the work the early spring.

When the work of drastic thinning and cutting back of a border is just completed, the general appearance before growth

A (*b*) 5 . . *Azara microphylla.*

E or D (*h*). . *Berberis aggregata, aristata, brevipaniculata, concinna, dictyophylla, Morrisonensis, Prattii, subcaulialata* and *Wisley* hybrids such as *rubrostilla, Sparkler* and *Winter Cheer.*

A (*g*) 4 . . *Berberis aquifolium.*

A . . . *Berberis candidula, Darwinii, Gagnepainii, Hookerii insignis, japonica* and varieties, *linearijolia, Sargentiana* and *stenophylla* (evergreen species).

A . . . *Berberis Thunbergii* and varieties, *atropurpurea* (deciduous).

D or E . . *Buddleia alternifolia.*

A (*g*) 5 . . *Buddleia globosa.*

B (*a*) 4 . . *Buddleia variabilis* and varieties, *magnifica, Veitchiana, Pink Pearl* and *nanhœnsis*; *B. Fallowiana.*

A (*b*) 4 . . *Callicarpa Geraldiana.*

(*l*) . . . *Calluna vulgaris* and varieties (heather).

A . . . *Calycanthus florida* and *occidentalis.*

A (*b*) 5 . . Camellias.

A (*b*) 5 . . *Carpentaria californica.*

A (*b*) (*g*) 5. . *Caryopteris mastacanthus, tangutica clandonensis.*

A (*b*) 5 . . *Cassinia fulvida* (syn. *Diplopappus chrysophyllus*).

A (*b*) 5 . . *Ceanothus azureus, Burkwoodii, dentatus, papillosus, rigidus* and *thyrsiflorus.*

B (*a*) 4 . . *Ceanothus* hybrids such as *Gloire de Versailles, Indigo, Perle Rose* and *Virginal.*

A (*b*) or (*c*) . *Ceratostigma Willmottianum.*

A . . . *Cercis siliquastrum* (Judas tree).

F, 2 . . . *Chimonanthus fragrans* (winter sweet).

A (*b*) 5 . . *Choisya ternata* (Mexican orange).

A . . . Cistus (rock rose).

A . . . *Clerodendron Fargesii, trichotomum.*

(*c*) . . . *Clerodendron foetidum.*

A . . . Colutea (bladder senna).

Above : *Moderate pruning of Buddleia variabilis. It would be possible to cut this bush much more severely if desired.*

Right : *Pruning side growths of a wall-trained Cydonia japonica. The shoot is being shortened to about five leaves.*

Pruning a Philadelphus after flowering. The old flowering wood is being removed.

Similar pruning of Forsythia suspensa. The cut has been made to young shoots.

Pruning a double-flowered Kerria japonica. In this case also the flowering wood is being shortened to a point from which a young shoot grows.

B (a) 4	. .	*Cornus alba* and varieties, *sibirica* and *Spæthii*; *C. stolonifera*.
A	. .	*Cornus capitata, florida* and varieties, *rubrea, Kousa* and varieties, *chinensis, Mas.*
A	. .	Corokias.
A (b) 4	. .	*Coronilla glauca* and *emerus*.
A	. .	*Corylopsis spicata*.
A	. .	Cotoneaster, all species and varieties.
A	. .	Cratægus (May).
F, 9	. .	Cydonias (flowering quince or 'japonica').
A (j) (k)	. .	Cytisus (brooms).
(l)	. .	*Dabœcia polifolia*.
A	. .	Daphnes.
A (b)	. .	*Decaisnea Fargesii*.
A (b)	. .	*Desfontainia spinosa*.
B, 1, 2, 3	. .	*Desmodium pendulifolium, ullæfolium*.
D or E (h)	.	Deutzias.
C	. .	Diervillas (weigela).
D or E	.	Dipeltas.
A	. .	Elæagnus.
A	. .	Enkianthus.
A (b)	. .	Erica (heath).
A (b)	. .	*Escallonia* Donard Seedling and varieties, *exoniensis, Iveyi, macrantha* and *rubra*.
D or E	.	*Escallonia langleyensis, edinensis, phillipiana*
A	. .	Eucryphias.
A (g) 1, 2, 3		Euonymus (spindle tree).
D or E	.	Exochordas.
A (b)	. .	*Fabiana imbricata* and *violacea*.
A (g) 1, 2, 3	.	*Forsythia intermedia, spectabilis* and *viridissima*.
C	. .	*Forsythia suspensa* and varieties *atrocaulis* and *Fortunei*.
A (b) 5	. .	Fremontias.
B or (a) or (b) 4		*Fuchsia coccinea, corallina, gracilis, globosa, macrostemma* and *Riccartonii*.
A	. .	*Garrya elliptica*.
A	. .	*Gaultheria Shallon* and *Veitchiana*.
B (a) 3	. .	*Genista tinctoria*.
A	. .	Genistas.

E

B, 3 . . .	Salix (willows), when grown as shrubs for stem beauty.
A (*f*) 1, 2, 3 .	Salix, weeping varieties.
B (*a*) 1, 2, 3 .	Sambucus (golden and variegated forms of elder).
A (*j*) . . .	*Senecio laxifolius* and *Grayii.*
A . . .	Skimmias.
A (*b*) (*f*) 5 .	*Solanum crispum jasminoides.*
(*m*) 3 . . .	*Spartium junceum* (Spanish broom).
B (*a*) 2, 3 . .	*Spiræa arborea, Aitchisonii, discolor (ariæfolia), Lindleyana.*
C . . .	*Spiræa arguta, Thunbergii.*
D or E . .	*Spiræa bracteata, canescens, Henryi, prunifolia, Reevesiana, van Houttei* and *Veitchii.*
B, 2, 3 . .	*Spiræa Bumalda, Anthony Waterer, japonica, margaritæ, Menziesii triumphans.*
A . . .	*Staphyleas colchica* and *pinnata* (bladder nut).
(*g*) 3 or (*c*) .	*Stephenandra Tanakæ* and *flexuosa.*
A . . .	Stewartias.
A . . .	*Stranvæsias Davidiana, undulata* and *salicifolia.*
A (*e*) . . .	*Styrax japonicum.*
E . . .	Symphoricarpus (snowberry).
A (*j*) (*k*) .	Syringa (lilac).
B (*a*) 1, 2, 3 .	*Tamarix pentandra* (syn. *hispida æstivalis*).
(*f*) 1, 2, 3 . .	*Tamarix tetrandra.*
A (*b*) . .	Veronicas.
A (*k*) . .	*Viburnum bitchuense, Carlesii.*
A . . .	*Viburnum Burkwoodii, fragrans, Davidii, Mariesii, plicatum, rhytidophyllum* and *Tinus.*
E (*h*) . . .	*Viburnum opulus sterile.*
A (*f*) 3 . .	Vinca (periwinkle).
(*f*) 4 . . .	Vitis (vines).
F (*f*) 8 . .	Wistaria.
A (*j*) . . .	*Zenobia speciosa* and *pulverulenta.*

CHAPTER SIX

PRUNING CLEMATIS

THE successful cultivation of clematis, in a large measure, depends upon an understanding of correct pruning. As a genus they vary in their mode of flowering, some doing so on young wood of current season's growth and others on shoots which were made the previous year. Many of them are not able sufficiently to ripen their wood to withstand the winter's cold and may, I suppose, only be considered as semi-woody subjects. It is important to remove wood which dies back in such cases regularly each year. Other kinds which must have regular pruning are those which tend to become bare at the base and produce a dense jungle of growth higher up if left to their own devices.

Clematis will undoubtedly continue to flower for many years if left unpruned, but the quality of flowers eventually deteriorates, and there is certain to be an accumulation of unwanted growth either dead or alive.

The area which each specimen is permitted to occupy, together with rigours of season and situation, are varying factors which to a large extent influence the extent of pruning.

The subject may appear complicated at first, although I have endeavoured to put it as simply as possible. As there are four different classes for discussion it has been necessary to give names of the more usual kinds in each, together with the group names assigned to them.

From the flowering point of view they may be divided into two sections, but from the pruning aspect each of these sections must again be divided, making four groups in all.

Section 1 consists of those varieties which flower on wood of the previous season's growth. They are:

Class One. Mostly comparatively small flowered kinds, many of which flower early in the season.

Class Two. For the most part these are larger flowered and are not early. Although flowering on similar wood to Class One they require different pruning.

Section 2 comprises the sorts which flower during the

CHAPTER SEVEN

THE PRUNING OF ROSES

ONCE roses are established under the best available conditions, more than half the battle in their successful cultivation lies in correct pruning. If this operation is neglected entirely, results are bound to be poor and the trees short-lived. If it is done incorrectly, flowering may be very poor and the trees will eventually become crippled.

Roses must be divided into various classes, but experience and acquaintanceship with the types and varieties are necessary before one can judge by inspection to which class a particular rose belongs. This is unfortunate, because each class requires a specialised form of pruning, and it is useless to inflict the same treatment upon a collection of different kinds. The only way out of the difficulty is to make a careful note of every variety of rose in the garden. Newly planted trees should be carefully labelled, and where old-established trees are not recognised, information should be sought from some expert.

It would be out of the question in this little book to give a classification of every known variety of rose. This information can easily be obtained from the catalogue of well-known rose specialists. Having then a list of all the varieties of roses in the garden, together with a catalogue giving classification, there should be little difficulty in ascertaining the particular method of pruning each requires.

I think it is important to remember the general principles connected with vigour and pruning when pruning roses. The more vigorous individuals should receive slightly less cutting, and, on the other hand, weaker ones should be rather more severely pruned. For very vigorous bush roses the method of pegging down shoots rather than cutting them, as discussed under the Hybrid Perpetuals, is strongly recommended.

Hybrid Teas.—Generally referred to as H.T. This section includes the majority of roses grown in gardens. Hybrid teas should be pruned about the end of March, cutting out all dead and worn-out wood. The weaker remaining young shoots should be pruned to within three or four buds of the old wood, whilst strong shoots should be pruned to a bud about 6 inches to 1 foot from their base according to comparative vigour. In every case cut to a bud facing outwards so as to keep the centre of the tree open. The same treatment applies for bushes and standards, excepting that even shape must be more considered in the latter, and it may be necessary to cut certain shoots either harder or more lightly than would otherwise be the case, in order to maintain an even balance of the tree. These remarks apply to roses for garden decoration. Where specimen blooms for exhibition are required, pruning must be much more severe. Weak growths are shortened to one bud, and stronger ones to two or at most three buds.

Popular examples of this class are *Betty Uprichard*, *Etoile de Hollande*, *Madame Butterfly*, *Ophelia* and *Shot Silk*. I think that there is little doubt concerning the treatment generally given to this class of rose by those who have not had much experience with them. The majority seem afraid to cut them severely enough, and as witness of this it is not necessary to look very far. Plants which were originally dwarf bushes have been allowed to grow much too tall by reason of an accumulation of old wood as a substructure, and each succeeding year the young flowering shoots are produced from a higher level. Not only do such bushes look untidy, but they lose their vitality.

Remember that bush roses flower on young wood and that such growth in strong and healthy condition is most willingly produced in response to hard pruning. Further than this, these young flowering shoots are seldom produced from old wood, but come from what is left of last year's wood after pruning is done, and what is most important the strongest will arise from the topmost buds left; that is to say, if pruning is but lightly done the flowering shoots are produced from the top, and the base of the shoot, which is quite unwanted, becomes bare and useless. It is sometimes possible to find a live bud or even a young shoot on the older wood at pruning time, when, of course, it is wise to cut back to it, but regard any shoot coming from the ground with suspicion, because it

Lancaster, is the best known. It is as well to cut them fairly hard at the end of March in the first season after planting. The same remarks apply to the varieties of *Rosa gallica*, which are the oldest roses of all known to European cultivation. *Rosa Mundi*, white striped pink, and *Tuscany* are the best known of these.

Rugosa Roses.—These tall-growing bush roses require no pruning when once established. They should be shortened back to within 6 inches of the ground at the end of March following planting and thereafter only cut when restriction becomes necessary.

Chinese Roses.—These are sometimes called Bengal roses, whilst some people know them as monthly roses on account of their constant bloom. They are only tolerably hardy and may require some attention to the removal of dead wood and the shortening back of shoots crippled by frost. Otherwise they require no pruning except during their first year, when all shoots should be cut back to half their length. Choose the first week in April for this work.

Sweet Briars.—The hybrid sweet briars, sometimes called Eglantine roses, are by nature vigorous subjects. They are generally used for screens, and I think they look at their best if left to grow naturally as an informal hedge. Grown in this way they would require no pruning beyond an occasional thinning out of the oldest wood. In cases where a formal or clipped hedge is required they may be trimmed in April, and again after flowering. This treatment will restrain flowering.

Dwarf Polyantha Roses.—These are represented by roses of the Poulsen type and the Orleans or true polyantha roses. They have now become very much the vogue for bedding or planting in mixed borders, and include the now well-known Poulsen family and also such varieties as *Coral Cluster*, *Edith Cavell*, *Gloria Mundi*, *Orleans* and *Yvonne Rabier*. They are very easy to prune. This work, which may be done from the middle to the end of March, consists of cutting out thin shoots, together with dead wood, and a brief shortening back of wood which it is decided to retain. Although I have said the work is simple, and by the description it will be seen to be lenient pruning, on no account omit to do it, or bushes will soon become overcrowded, leggy, and show a marked decrease in vigour and flowering capabilities.

Climbing Roses.—There can be very few gardens where climbing roses of some kind or another are not represented. There are several types, all requiring different treatment, and, unfortunately, as most pergolas or fences are planted with a collection of varying types, the pruning becomes involved. Further than this there has been much hybridising between the various classes, and it is not always easy to decide into which section a particular variety belongs. Pruning is essential for every kind and I will endeavour to simplify the subject as far as possible.

Climbing Hybrid Teas.—These are mostly represented by varieties with large flowers resembling those of dwarf bush roses. In fact, many of them are vigorous forms of well-known bush varieties. For example, *Climbing Madame Butterfly*, or *Climbing Lady Hillingdon*, are merely strong growing sports of the bush types, and are identical in appearance except for degree of vigour. Others have no dwarf counterpart and are really just vigorous H.T. roses suitable for climbing only. These are represented by such varieties as *Gruss an Teplitz*, *Lemon Pillar* and *Paul's Carmine Pillar*. There should be no difficulty in recognising these roses, and it is important to do so, because they must be pruned lightly. Hard cutting always brings an excess of vigour with very little flower production, and this is an instance where light pruning in the season after planting is recommended.

Pruning should be done in the middle of March in sheltered positions such as against the house or a wall, but in the open on a post may be deferred for a week. Remove all dead wood, shorten any weak shoots to about three buds, and merely tip strong shoots to remove any unripened wood. There are a few varieties which may be listed in some catalogues as climbing tea roses, such as *Climbing Lady Hillingdon* and *Tea Rambler*, but the treatment is identical.

Climbing Noisettes.—These are similar to the climbing H.T.s although they are not so hardy and produce their flowers in clusters. Such well-known sorts as *Madame A. Carriere*, *Marechal Niel* and *William Allen Richardson* are included. It is important to distinguish them from the climbing

It is important to prune all rambler roses as soon after flowering as possible, so that the wood which is retained may be tied into position early, and thus receive the benefit of late summer and autumn sunshine to promote thorough ripening.

Weeping Standards.—These are actually varieties of rambler roses which have been propagated by budding on to an alien stock. They should be pruned in exactly the same way as ordinary ramblers. Some people like to train them over special wire supports, in which case young shoots must be tied down before they have become rigid at an unwanted angle. At the same time, it is not advisable to shorten any of this growth when the old wood is taken out after flowering, but to wait until the following spring.

Suckers.—Most types of roses may be readily propagated from cuttings, in which case any young shoots appearing from beneath ground level may be treated as part of the plant itself. Unfortunately, with the exception of ramblers and types such as Rugosa and Provence roses, cuttings are not always consistent with long life. Nurserymen therefore bud or graft most of their roses on to stocks, or rooting systems, of wild briar or other types. Bush and standard roses of all kinds, climbing H.T.s and H.P.s, are therefore not growing upon their own roots. These stock roots often send up shoots of their own, which must be immediately removed or else they will deprive the legitimate plant of some of its energy. There can be no doubt about distinguishing a sucker in that it will be of different growth and with an unmatched foliage to that of the planted variety.

Summer Pruning Bush Roses.—All H.T. and H.P. roses give their best display during June. They also give a second flowering during the autumn months. A great deal can be done to enhance the latter if a light pruning is done as soon as the first blossoming is over. Shorten back the young wood beneath the faded flowers by as much as half its length. This not only obviates seed formation, which in itself is an exhausting process, but encourages a reinvigoration of the whole plant with a consequent production of more young growth which provides the autumn blossoms.

Stages in the hard pruning of an H.T. rose. In the uppermost illustration the bush is seen before pruning, in the middle all unwanted wood has been removed, while at the bottom the remaining wood has been shortened severely.

A typical H.T. bush rose before pruning.

Useless growth is removed right to the base.

The three remaining good shoots are pruned moderately for garden display.

Pruning roots of a bush rose prior to planting.

A cluster of rose-buds before dis-budding.

The same rose stem after removal of surplus buds.

Removing side shoots and tendrils from cordon-trained sweet peas.

Removing side buds from a dahlia grown for exhibition.

Left: A rambler rose of the Dorothy Perkins type before pruning. The photograph was taken immediately after flowering.

Right: The same rose after removal of old flowering wood right to the base. Young shoots which have not yet flowered are being trained to the rustic screen.

CHAPTER EIGHT

PRUNING APPLES AND PEARS

It is a sufficiently difficult matter to demonstrate, to those who are anxious to learn, the principles which embody the successful pruning of apples and pears. Trees vary so much in shape and vigour, whilst individual varieties all have different characteristics. It is even more difficult to write upon the subject in such a way as to give clear-cut instructions. There can be no rule-of-thumb pruning of these subjects, because it is necessary to study the individuality of each tree before deciding how to treat it.

Unquestionably the most important factor in the successful cultivation of these fruits lies in vigour control; that is to say, everything possible must be done to strike a happy medium between a stunted tree making little or no young wood each year, and an overvigorous habit where the tree produces masses of very long whippy shoots. The tree of moderate vigour should produce a reasonable amount of young wood each year, and these young shoots vary in length from 6 inches to 2 or 3 feet. The first aim must be, then, to produce this happy state of affairs, because not only will pruning become a simple matter, but there is every likelihood of regular bearing of good crops.

Vigour control is so important, and is connected so intimately with pruning, that I have no hesitation in embarking briefly on the subject of cultivation. This will show how vigour may be increased or reduced.

To Increase Vigour.

(a) By feeding either with a complete plant food such as manure or compost, or a proprietary inorganic fertiliser, but primarily by the use of nitrogenous fertilisers such as sulphate of ammonia or nitro chalk.

(b) By watering and mulching.

(c) By good cultivation over the roots of the tree.

(d) By hard pruning. This will consist of cutting out any unwanted or overcrowded branches for a start. But by far the most invigorating effect will be produced by a complete cutting away of a large proportion of fruit spurs, together with a drastic thinning of fruit buds on those spurs which are retained. At the same time, when doing this work be careful as far as is possible to retain any young wood which may have been produced the previous season. The presence of short young shoots in this instance are an aid to the strength of the tree in that they produce strong foliage. These healthy leaves are important in the plant's food manufacturing process.

(e) By thinning the crop. Very stunted trees are unlikely to produce much fruit unless they have rested for one or two seasons previously. The extent to which the crop is thinned must depend upon the tree's response to its treatment. If by July a reasonable amount of growth has appeared this need not be severe, but if it is still obviously in an emaciated condition very little fruit should be left.

(f) (For oblique cordons only.) By carefully raising the trees and tying them in at a less acute angle. This has a marked stimulating effect.

To Reduce Vigour.

(a) By root pruning or ringing.

(b) By ceasing cultivation over the roots of the tree, or, better still, by grassing down this area.

(c) By very light pruning. This involves the most important principle in pruning, which I shall discuss fully later on. The most certain way to check vigour is to make the tree produce fruit, and the unquestionable means of doing this is to leave as much young wood on the tree as possible.

(d) (For younger trees.) By bending down some of the lower retained shoots to encourage fruit bud formation.

(e) (For oblique cordons only.) By tying the trees down to a sharper angle. They may be returned to their previous position when the desired effect has been accomplished. I have definite proof of the potency of this method. Fifteen years ago I planted over three acres of cordon apples and pears, and for the first few years there was great trouble in controlling growth. The trees were on dwarfing stock (Type 2), but the soil was too good. All trees were taken down from the wires where they had been tied at an angle of 45 degrees and sloped down to nearly 30 degrees. The plantation was also grassed down. Within two seasons they were fruiting heavily and were returned to their original position. The fruiting had brought them to heel and their over-exuberance had disappeared.

Pruning for Shape.—The shape of a tree, or its actual formation, is a matter of significant importance. I do not refer to cordons and espaliers in the sense that while everyone likes to see them neatly trained, sun and air can reach all parts of them. But not so with bush and standard trees which have been given unmindful treatment. It is essential that sun and air should be able to reach every part of the tree. This prevents disease, not only of the fruit but of the tree itself. It adds colour, size and flavour to the fruit, and also means that it will be successfully produced on the inside as well as the outside of the branches. The centre of these trees must therefore be open.

All sorts of objects have been borrowed to describe the shape of the ideal tree, including funnels, wine glasses and inverted umbrellas. The classical tree should, I suppose, resemble one or other of these objects. It should have about eight to twelve main branches, which should be fairly straight and regularly spaced, all radiating outwards, not so steeply as to shut in the centre of the tree, and not so widely angled that a heavy crop will either smash them or pull them down to the horizontal.

It is very satisfying and quite simple, too, to produce trees answering this description if responsibility is taken for them from their childhood, but pruning has often to be tackled on trees which have received indifferent treatment in their younger days. However, this will not affect the quality of fruit if the centre of the tree is opened. The saw should immediately be taken to all trees with crowded centres, and all branches which grow inwards, or in fact in the centre, should be cut out. Conversely straggling branches should be dealt with. If there is another branch in the same plane, above one which is bowed down, the latter can be cut out, but if there is not, it may be possible to pull it up into position and secure by means of a stout stake.

I do not like to see branches which cross one another. This means for certain that some part of one of the branches is not going to get a fair share of light. Moreover, if the higher one is heavily cropped it is liable to bend down so that it rubs against the one beneath, and a wound follows which is a direct invitation for canker to gain an entrance, with a possible risk of losing both branches.

It is frequently possible to cut back a branch by only a portion of its length in order to accomplish improvement in shape. In such cases the cut is carefully made to a promising young shoot pointing in the correct direction.

Another point to bear in mind is that whilst it is never wise to delay in cutting out branches which are choking the centre of the tree, others which are badly placed may be with advantage left for a twelvemonth if they are well covered with fruit buds. Make a mental note that the branch must come out next year, and in the meantime search for the young shoot which represents the infancy of the new branch and see that it is but lightly pruned. Thus you will benefit by the fruit from the condemned branch, and at the same time have already started to form its better placed successor.

One simple tip in connection with sawing branches. I am no expert carpenter, and have very often found the saw only too willing to travel on as it comes through the branch on its last cut and do damage to spurs or wanted shoots beneath. I now always hold my sécateurs (closed) immediately beneath the branch and in the passage of the saw so as to prejudice its unwelcome activities. It may seem a small point, but unnecessary wounds of any kind are inexcusable. Always finish off saw cuts with a sharp knife so as to leave a smooth wound, and paint them over with neat tar-oil wash, Stockholm tar or 'Medo'. After a few seasons' use I have found the last named to be an excellent disinfectant and a deterrent to canker.

The Removal of Dead and Diseased Wood.—This axiomatic instruction must not be overlooked. The only diseases which are likely to be troublesome are canker and scab. The latter attacks foliage, fruit (spotting and craking) and young shoots, and on varieties which are susceptible may be detected on young wood which has a blistered appearance. Unfortunately, canker often follows in the footsteps of scab, so that it really is important to watch out and remove scab-damaged wood.

Canker is an unpleasant complaint especially encountered

in badly drained orchards. If left unchecked it soon encompasses the branch attacked. A main stem or branch entirely begirt has received its death sentence. Young shoots or spurs with canker should always be cut out. With branches, if more than two-thirds of the circumference is attacked fetch them out because they are not worth saving. If less than two-thirds, either carefully cut the canker out, being certain to go on cutting until sound wood is reached, and then paint over, or apply 'Medo' without performing the operation.

Brown rot is another disease which causes a big loss in apples and pears, the fruit going, as the name implies, brown and rotten. When pruning, look out for the small, hard, shrivelled fruits still on the trees, which harbour the disease in a dormant state. They sometimes rest in spurs, when the disease may attack the wood and buds, and it will be quite evident if it has done so. This wood must be removed.

All dead and diseased wood of any kind should be burnt.

I have now discussed three important and vital points which must be applied in the consideration of correct pruning. Dead and diseased wood must be cut out, the shape of the tree, together with the opening out of the centre, taken into consideration, and finally, and most important of all, the degree of vigour of the tree noted, so that the measure of pruning may be reconcilable with strength of growth.

Pruning Established Bush Trees.—There can be no question now that in the past these trees have been much too severely pruned, not only in private gardens but in commercial orchards as well. Almost everyone who tended their trees well used to shorten back young shoots to about 6 inches in length in summer and the following winter cut right back to the fruit bud or buds which were formed upon it. This was spur pruning, and was, I think, subject to slight variations, the generally accepted practice. Trees used to look very neat and trim, with their short spurs set all along the branches, and when pruning was done there was not a great deal of young wood left on the tree, with the possible exception of the leaders (these are the shoots which form the prolongation of the main branches, and also shoots which are selected as being well placed to form an additional branch). It was the method recommended in the first two editions of this book, and judging from observation is still generally employed in most private gardens.

Now this system has grave drawbacks, and it has taken a long time to discover this fact. Firstly, it limits cropping capability. Secondly, it tends to encourage a biennial bearing habit, and thirdly, if a branch became broken, or badly bent out of position by a heavy crop, it took many seasons to train up another to replace it. Finally, if a tree was at all vigorous the condition was merely aggravated and thickets of young wood were produced instead of fruit buds.

Modern practice recommends a much lighter pruning. In Chapter Two I was at some pains to explain how that young wood is a potential source of fruiting wood. Let us see how that wood can best be utilised to supply maximum and regular crops. The aim should be to leave as much young wood on the tree as possible without causing overcrowding, at the same time removing types of young shoots which are undesirable. The unwanted ones will be those which are weak and spindly, and also those very strong growths known as 'water shoots' which sometimes spring from the main trunk or low down in the forks of branches. All these may be removed completely.

All remaining young shoots, with the exception of the leaders, are laterals. There will have to be varying degrees of shortening these, ranging from 2 inches to leaving them at practically full length. The whole operation is one of thinning and spacing so that none of the retained laterals are close to each other and none of them must be allowed to cross or touch. The higher the position in the tree, the farther apart branches become, and the more space to leave laterals. In positions where it is found possible to leave them at almost full length no two laterals should be closer than 1 foot to each other. Even at the top of some branches it will be found necessary to shorten some to 6 inches or so, in order to leave room for others left at a greater length.

Where trees have been habitually hard pruned in the past a lot of the young wood will be found to be growing away from existing fruit spurs. Providing these spurs are stocky and well formed there is no objection to leaving such laterals fairly long. But in cases where the spur is very old and badly formed it would be better to dispense with the entire spur and shoot and wait for a year for a strong new lateral which will appear from the branch as compensation.

Whilst this work is proceeding, attention must be given to the fruit spurs themselves. If these are aged and are getting worn out and extended, cut them right out. One obviously cannot remove all the spurs even on very neglected trees, but cut out one or two of the worst on each branch. Other spurs may be healthy but overcrowded, in which case they must be reduced in size, more especially on weak growing branches.

The following winter all the young shoots which have been left, and especially those which were left fairly long, will be found to be carrying a large number of fruit buds, as well as one or more shoots at the top. They may either be shortened back to a fruit bud high up on the original shoot (there should be a few fruit buds beneath it), so that you are leaving, say, four or five fruit buds, or if you think there is room to extend a little further, cut into the young wood produced at the top of the original, leaving it a further 6 or 9 inches long.

In some cases, especially in very vigorous trees, it may be found that perhaps only one fruit bud has formed and that the remaining ones are only half formed; that is to say, they are developing fruit buds. It will take another year for them to complete formation, and this work will be done more readily if the original shoot is not cut but left at the same length, whilst growths produced from the top of it may be shortened as desired and according to space available.

So the process goes on each year. Remove one or two of the older spurs entirely; leave the best placed young shoots as long as possible; thin out altogether the weak shoots and short unproductive stubs, and treat those laterals which were left the previous year as I have described.

The system is not easy to describe in words, but the accompanying illustrations should be of great assistance in following the operations. Its great advantages lie in the continued rejuvenation of the tree. Fruit is continually being born on two- or three-year-old wood, and this fruit is of the finest quality. Moreover, the total cropping capacity is vastly increased. Another considerable advantage is that there is always a large supply of potential new branches. When pruning time comes, room may well be found for some of the two-year-old growths (the original shoot left at full length plus the wood it made last summer), and indeed some of them may be better placed than the branch from which they were produced. In this case they would be left at almost full length for a second year in succession and the unwanted portion of the original branch removed. I always make a practice of trying to visualise the position of each branch as it will be when bearing heavily. This is easily done by pulling gently but firmly downwards. If the branch is at all weak or lying lower than it should, look for the replacement shoot coming from lower down on that branch and straight away tip that shoot to a bud near its extremity and pointing in the correct direction.

All leaders, and potential leaders, should be pruned to a bud pointing in the desired direction. The severity with which they should be cut depends on the vigour of the tree. In healthy trees they need only be tipped, but where growth is indifferent follow the general principle to prune hard to increase vigour.

I have said rather a lot about this system of pruning, which is excusable as it is in a measure a contradiction of what I wrote fifteen years ago. I think that the crux of the matter lies in the fact that with the old-fashioned hard spurring all went well until the tree was under the strain of a heavy crop combined with drought conditions; that is to say, that each individual spur was unable to carry its fruit and to make new fruit buds for next year's crop at the same time. Now this new method allows for a large amount of young wood, besides long and short spurs at the same time on the tree. It is much more easy and more natural for the tree to convert the growth buds on this young wood into fruit buds during the coming season than it is for it to make fresh fruit buds on the old spurs. The system therefore makes ample provision for regular bearing, but it will be clear that this can only be accomplished in conjunction with reasonable care in cultivation which assures that the tree continues to make healthy growth year by year.

Biennial Bearing.—There are certain excellent varieties

which are prone to produce a crop one year and to rest the next. I am not referring to trees which are scarcely sufficiently well fed, which will generally fall into this habit, but to sorts which appear disposed towards biennial bearing under good cultivation. The worst offenders in my experience are *Ellison's Orange*, *Laxton's Superb*, *King of the Pippins*, *Miller's Seedling* and *Newton Wonder*.

To counteract this tendency prune young wood especially lightly, but remove a generous proportion of the existing fruit buds before the 'on' year (when heavy crops are anticipated). Conversely, cut the young wood a trifle more severely than usual before the 'off' year, shortening about one-third of the laterals to about 2 inches. At the same time short laterals of from 4 to 6 inches in length, with a terminal fruit bud, should have this bud removed by tipping before the 'on' year, but it should be retained prior to the 'off' year.

A little thought will show that the reasons for these instructions are very feasible. Light pruning is recommended before the 'on' year so as to leave a considerable amount of young wood on the tree to give it every opportunity of converting it into fruiting wood for the season after. That is to say, it is encouraged to form fruit buds for next year, which would normally be the 'off' year. The heavier pruning is done prior to the 'off' year to encourage growth. This means that in twelve months' time, when pruning is once again being done prior to the 'on' season, the tree is well furnished with young wood, which is just what is wanted.

Tip Fruiting Varieties.—I referred a few paragraphs back to lateral growths with a terminal fruit bud. This is a common enough thing, especially after a dry summer. There are certain varieties which do not form fruit spurs very happily if subjected to routine pruning, but which prefer to specialise in making short side growths with a terminal fruit bud to each. If a lot of cutting of laterals is done on these subjects they produce very little fruit. The best way to treat them is to make as few cuts into young wood as possible, but to attend to the shape of the tree by making a few large cuts each winter. Varieties in this section are *Blenheim Orange*, *Bramley's Seedling*, *Devonshire Quarrenden*, *Cornish Gilliflower*, *Irish Peach* and *Worcester Pearmain*.

Dehorning.—No book on pruning would be complete without mentioning this process. It is a method used by commercial growers for dealing with neglected trees and consists of drastic cutting out of entire branches. I suppose in a measure I have already described the operation whilst stressing the importance of keeping the centre of the tree open. If ever you are sufficiently unfortunate to be confronted with that all too common type of tree found in gardens, which has come under the lash of the sécateur fiend for years on end and represents a pollarded street tree, and with spurs looking like osier stumps after trimming, try this method. Remove entirely the overcrowding branches, reduce the number of spur stumps on the retained branches, and thin out the young wood on the remaining spurs. But leave as much young wood as possible without overcrowding, and those shoots which you do keep, leave at almost full length.

Building up a Bush Tree.—An excellent method of making a small orchard is to purchase one-year-old or 'maiden' trees from the nursery and to build up the trees in your own garden. A maiden consists of a single shoot from 3 to 5 feet in length. The maidens, having been planted, should be cut back to a bud at approximately knee height. Now it is not desirable that this top bud should make strong growth, because its shoot would continue to grow upwards into what would be the centre of the tree. Discourage it, therefore, by making a little nick in the bark immediately beneath the bud, using a sharp knife for the purpose. Now select three buds in the 6 inches of stem below the nick. These buds are to produce shoots which will form the first three branches of the tree. For this reason choose healthy-looking buds, and three which radiate outwards at approximately equal angles; that is to say, one bud might be facing north-west, another due east and the third a trifle west of south. Encourage these buds to grow strongly by making a little notch in the bark immediately above them. It is useful to remember at all times when training trees that a nick beneath a bud discourages it to grow and a notch above has the reverse effect.

At the end of the growing season there should be three nice shoots growing out at the desired angle and about 2 feet in length. When pruning time arrives, cut away everything above the topmost of the three shoots. The central 'stump' has now served its purpose of encouraging outward growth beneath it, and is of no further use. Also remove any other superfluous shoots which may have appeared besides the three which are required. These three should now be shortened back by about half their length. The ideal would be for them each to produce two strong shoots so that the tree will be provided with six young branches. Bearing this in mind, it may be useful to employ a notch on each of the three pruned shoots. The bud to which the pruning cut is made will produce one strong shoot, and this should be selected as a bud pointing in the desired direction. The second shoot may be encouraged by employing a notch.

The following winter there should be the solid basis of a young tree. Clean up the stem between the ground level and the lowest of the three original branches by entire removal of any shoots which may have appeared. Side shoots or 'laterals' from the foot length retained of the original three branches should be thinned and those retained shortened (or spurred) to between 4 and 6 inches, and the leaders or six main branches shortened by about half their length, and always to a bud pointing in the most advantageous direction.

The next winter a few fruit buds will have appeared on the spurred laterals. Cut back to the fruit buds. Again spur laterals on the two-year-old wood and treat the leaders as before. Up to the present, pruning has been severe in order to encourage growth and to build up a strong framework, which is the only way to form the foundation of a satisfactory tree. By this time the tree should be expressing its individuality. If it is strong growing, pruning must be lighter, and there must be a gradual change over to the methods described for established bush trees. If, on the contrary, growth is weak, continue with severe pruning and apply the methods recommended for inducing vigour earlier in this chapter.

Pruning of Transplanted Three- to Five-Year-Olds.—After many years experimenting I am firmly convinced that it pays to build up a tree by planting it at as early a stage as possible in its permanent quarters. In the orchard which I have established, the bush trees which were planted as maidens, spaced at the appropriate distance (in this instance 12 feet apart each way), have made the best trees with the least trouble.

Where trees up to five years old are planted, pruning for the first few seasons must be severe to encourage growth. The reader is referred to the notes on pruning at planting time, and thereafter for the next two or three seasons strongly advised to encourage healthy growth before thinking about fruit production. Planting old trees with a view to obtaining immediate fruit is an unwise procedure. Always build up a strong tree first, and then gradually transfer to lighter pruning and heavy crops.

Standard Trees.—The head of a standard tree should be formed in precisely the same way as that recommended for bush trees, the only difference being the length of stem, which is round about 6 feet for a standard and 18 inches less for a half-standard. Once the shape of the tree is well formed with a good open centre, very little further pruning is necessary. Now and again it may be found advisable to remove a branch which is found either growing towards the centre or crossing one of its neighbours.

Summer Pruning.—Summer pruning is an operation which consists of shortening back wood of the current season's growth of laterals (but not leaders) during July and August. I do not recommend it for bush or standard trees which are established. In the case of very vigorous young trees it is a good plan to shorten laterals to 6 or 8 inches in length during July. This checks the vigour of the trees, assists in the formation of the shape, and permits the sun to get into the centre of the tree to ripen off wood which is to be retained.

Cordons.—The successful cultivation of cordons is by no means a simple matter, and no degree of skilful pruning can compensate for certain other factors. By virtue of its formation and intensive planting the cordon tree must be made to produce its fruit on closely formed spurs. This can only be done successfully if, firstly, only varieties which respond to hard spur pruning are selected, and secondly, the vigour of the tree is fully under control. I mention these facts because certain varieties of apple, notably *Bramley's Seedling* and *Worcester Pearmain*, are sometimes planted as cordons, and there can be no genuine recommendation for pruning them because they are not suitable varieties for this form of culture. Again, trees planted on stocks other than dwarfing ones (Type 2 for lighter soils or Type 9 for richer ones) are certain to become overvigorous, and the only remedy is to treat them as recommended in the notes on vigour control. This is because, with the cordon, there can be no safety valve for excessive vigour of very light pruning. Fruit must be borne within 6 inches of the main stem, otherwise the principle of the system is defeated and either bushes or dwarf pyramids might just as well have been planted.

The building up of a cordon tree from a maiden is simplicity itself. No pruning at all is done during the winter in which it is planted. The next winter leave the leader untouched, and side shoots on the original maiden length should be shortened to 6 inches. During the following winter again leave the leader unpruned. The laterals which were shortened the previous year on the now three-year-old part of the tree will almost certainly have produced fruit buds, and should be cut back into the old wood so as to leave only two of these buds, thus forming a permanent fruit spur. At the same time side shoots on the now two-year-old wood are shortened to 6 inches. The process is continued in this way, spurring laterals each year to 6 inches and then cutting back to the fruit buds formed on them the following year. In cases where a pruned lateral has not produced fruit buds within a twelvemonth, it will certainly have produced some developing fruit buds and some side shoots. Shorten these side shoots to within two buds of the original lateral and by the following winter the fruit buds will have fully developed, and the spur is formed in the same way as previously by cutting them back.

When the cordon has attained its required length one of two things may be done. In the case of oblique cordons the leader may be left unpruned and the whole tree tied down to a sharper angle. I have seen cordons over fifty years of age with the leaders still growing unpruned, the trees being 30 feet long. I do not like this method, because it brings the tops of the trees so close together. My own practice is to stop the tree when it is as long as required by cutting back the leader each year. Trained at an angle of 45 degrees the tops of the trees are as far apart as the base, and every fruit gets its fair share of sunshine.

The pruning of established cordons is simple providing the correct varieties have been chosen and the trees have not been allowed to become overvigorous. I think there should be slight differentiation according to variety.

(a) Those which form fruit buds with great ease and respond to very hard cutting. With these varieties there should be a hard thinning out of fruit buds on each spur, and it is a simple matter to keep the spurs very compact by shortening them annually. Three or four buds on each spur are sufficient to leave. *Beauty of Bath* and *James Grieve* fall into this category.

(b) Those which form fruit buds quite readily, but which in my experience are better for slightly less severe cutting. I thin out the buds on each spur in the same way as class (a), but the young wood produced from these spurs, instead of being cut right out, is shortened back to two buds if they are healthy wood, and cut right out if they are thin. Thus, when pruning is finished each spur should be furnished with about four or five fruit buds, and about three stumps of young wood shortened to two buds. In this class I place *Charles Ross*, *Cox's Orange Pippin*, *Ellison's Orange* and *Rival*.

(c) *Laxton's Superb* should be considered in a class by itself. It is the only other dessert apple worth growing as a cordon, but it is difficult to manage so as to make it crop every year. The best way is to treat it in exactly the same way as class (b), only to leave only one or two young shoots on each spur and these much longer, certainly not less than 4 inches. The following winter cut back to the fruit bud or buds formed on this young wood. It is useless to try to hard spur this variety, and some young wood must be left each year. When spurs have grown too long I cut them right out and replace them by shortening back the best placed of the fresh young shoots (which will undoubtedly appear in place of the removed spur) to 6 inches, and waiting for the fruit buds as in the original cordon pruning discussed.

All the above varieties should occasionally have the worst shaped of their spurs entirely cut out. All of them will respond with fresh young wood for the making of a new spur. *Ellison's Orange* is the only exception, and with this variety it is safer to shorten a worn-out spur to a dormant bud rather than cut it right out.

So far only dessert apples have been mentioned, although *Charles Ross* is, of course, a dual-purpose variety. Where it is wished to plant cooking sorts as cordons, *Emneth Early* and *Monarch* should be selected. Both these varieties produce fruit buds with great freedom and may be hard spurred.

Among pears, almost all varieties are suitable for cordons and may be relied upon to produce spurs and fruit buds with great ease. They should therefore be hard spurred. The only exception in my experience is *Pitmaston Duchess*. I planted one hundred cordons of this variety some years ago and have since regretted the choice. It is quite as difficult as *Laxton's Superb* apple and as a variety is not worth the trouble, whereas the apple undoubtedly is.

I have given rather rule-of-thumb instructions for the pruning of cordons. I have spent some time on this type of tree over the last fifteen years and am well satisfied with the results obtained. The instructions given will not apply to neglected or overvigorous trees which are almost impossible to prune satisfactorily, and because of the extreme importance of the point, and because it is so much bound up with pruning, I would like once again to emphasise the necessity of full control over the vigour of these trees.

Espaliers.—The pruning of espalier-trained apples and pears and the selection of varieties suitable for the purpose may be taken as precisely the same as suggested for cordons. The only practical point which arises is that the leaders of each horizontal branch, instead of being left unpruned, should be tipped to a bud facing downwards. This will assist in training the branches in a straight line and counteract the natural tendency of the shoot to grow upwards.

Summer Pruning Cordons and Espaliers.—Summer pruning is a very simple operation in that it consists merely of shortening back young wood of the current season's growth during July and August. Since the shoots which are cut will have to be further shortened back in the winter there is no need to make the actual cut to a bud. The purpose of the operation is to provide a temporary check to the growth of the tree, thereby assisting in maturing the fruit. It also allows the sun to reach the fruit, thereby improving its colour. It is also frequently claimed that summer pruning assists in fruit bud formation. This is a difficult thing to prove, but there can be no doubt that the admission of light and air assists in ripening off those fruit buds which in any case are in process of formation. The best time to carry out the operation is about one month before the fruit is ready for picking.

Where trees are exceptionally vigorous it is a good plan to summer prune about the middle of June. Shoots which are shortened at this time of the year are almost certain to throw out strong secondary growth, which should in turn be well shortened back one month later. If trees, on the other hand, are making poor growth, it is better not to summer prune. Let them form every leaf possible to aid fruit production and general well-being.

When to Winter Prune.—I suppose there is a 'best time' for winter pruning, which is when the trees are quite dormant. This would be from the middle of November when all leaves have dropped until the end of February before buds have started to break. If you have a lot of apples and pears to prune there is no reason at all why the work should not be started at the beginning of November and extended until the end of April, and certainly no harm will befall the tree. When late pruning is carried out, as it often has to be in commercial orchards, care must be taken of the swelling fruit buds, which are very brittle and apt to rub off at the slightest touch.

Dwarf Pyramids.—The dwarf pyramid is a comparatively new departure in apple and pear culture and has been evolved as a method of intensive culture which eliminates the necessity of supports required by cordons and espaliers.

The typical dwarf pyramid, when fully grown, is about 8 feet in height and is cone-shaped. There is a straight central stem from ground level to the tip of the tree from which radiate horizontal branches from all sides. These side branches are never allowed to grow more than 18 inches long so that the trees may be planted at 3 feet apart in rows which need not be more than 6 feet apart.

I must again refer to the question of vigour control which is essential if these trees are to be successfully grown. As soon as the tree has reached its full size, which has been described,

Above : Looking down from above on a well-formed bush apple to show the radiating branches and open centre.

Right : The same tree seen from the side. Note particularly the even spacing of the branches and the good balance of the whole tree. Variety, Cox's Orange Pippin.

Left : A young bush apple tree before summer pruning.

Right : The same tree after correct summer pruning, designed to maintain the good shape of the tree and preserve an open centre.

Left: A cordon apple tree pruned on the Lorette system. Brindles have been tied downwards to check the flow of sap and encourage formation of fruit buds

Right: A close-up of a section of a branch pruned on the Lorette system. Note the fruit buds forming on very short spurs.

Above: Side growths on Apple Laxton's Superb pruned on the modified Lorette system. Each has been cut back to one bud above the basal rosette of leaves.

Left: A more general view of the same tree showing the result of this pruning in an abundant crop of apples. The fruit gets full sun and "finishes" well.

there must be provision for checking a continuance of excessive vigour, otherwise correct pruning will become impossible. The usual method is to grass down the plantation, and this is to be preferred to ringing.

In order to build up a dwarf pyramid from a maiden it must be cut back during the first season of planting to a height of about 2 feet. This is generally done fairly late in the season to make certain of cutting to a healthy bud. During the summer do not prune the top shoot, but as soon as side shoots have reached a length of about 1 foot shorten them back to 6 inches. The next winter (twelve months after planting) the top shoot must be pruned to within 9 inches of the first cut, so that the tree will now be 2 feet 9 inches tall. In order to compensate for any slight deviation in the erect, choose a bud pointing in the correct direction. This will generally be found to be one on the opposite side of the stem to that which was selected during the first winter. At the same time any secondary growth which has appeared on the summer pruned laterals should be cut away.

During the second summer all laterals must as before be shortened to half their length as soon as they have made 1 foot of growth. It will be impossible to do this in one operation and the trees must be frequently inspected. Do not summer prune the leading shoot.

During the second winter again shorten the leading shoot so that only 9 inches of young wood is left, once again taking care to select the bud pointing in the direction to make the main stem quite straight. In pruning the laterals, which will now be more numerous in number, especially towards the base of the tree, a certain amount of thought will be necessary in order to maintain the perfectly shaped tree. There must be a tendency to remove entirely shoots which grow either inwards or upwards, and to train the extremities of the horizontal fruiting spurs in a slightly downward direction by pruning to a shoot pointing in the desired direction.

When the pyramid has reached full size, or just before if it is at all vigorous, attention must be given to check growth in the manner already suggested. The method of pruning throughout remains similar, bearing especially in mind to restrict the final length of all horizontal spurs to 18 inches.

G

their utmost to encourage as high a percentage of production as possible.

I have given the system a fair trial over several seasons upon a few cordon trees and have not been impressed with results. There is, however, a modified form of Lorette pruning, which will be described later, which is now being extensively used in cordon orchards, and is not only giving very successful results, but enables a great deal of work which would otherwise be done in winter to be carried out during August and September.

The Lorette system appears somewhat complicated at first, although its originator claims it to be 'childishly simple'. Certain terms which have not appeared elsewhere in this book have to be used, and it would be as well to start with a few definitions.

(1) *Fruiting Lateral.*—Short-branched side growths which give rise to one or more fruit spurs. These latter should bear fruit regularly each season.

(2) *Dart.*—A very short growth with a terminal bud. Lorette refers to it as the intermediary stage between an eye (or bud) and a fruit bud.

(3) *Stipulary Buds.*—Are those which are produced at the very base of young shoots. They appear in the axils of the stipules (or small leaves). They are less conspicuous and not so vigorous as ordinary buds.

(4) *Fruit Spurs.*—Short growths producing one or more fruit buds. They originate from shoots which have been pruned. They differ from fruiting laterals in that the latter originate from naturally formed flower buds.

(5) *Brindles.*—These are weaker growing fruiting laterals and are those shoots, and eventually small branches, which never attain the thickness of a pencil. It is important to distinguish between the two types, as they must receive different treatment.

The Lorette System in Practice.—The basic difference between the Lorette and other systems of pruning is that the former sets out to develop the stipulary buds, which under the more customary practice would most likely remain dormant throughout the life of the tree. The system may briefly be summarised as follows: Leaders are pruned at the end of April or beginning of May. Remaining shoots are pruned when they are half woody during June, July and August.

Treatment of Leaders.—Leaders, as has been mentioned, are pruned when the sap is rising. M. Lorette suggests that the work should be done when the young side shoots produced from them are approximately 2 inches long. He gives as outside dates for this operation 20th April until 5th May. For the most part leaders must be lightly pruned, especially with vigorous trees. Approximately one-quarter of the total length should be removed. In shady positions pruning should be more severe.

Formation of Fruiting Laterals.—It has already been defined that fruiting laterals appear from naturally formed fruit buds. These are formed on the portion of the leader which remains unpruned, either in the first or second year following pruning. These fruiting laterals must be encouraged in their continued production of fruit and fruit buds for the following season by means of severe summer pruning. It is maintained that this severe pruning directs the sap not only to the fruit but also to the swelling fruit buds.

Treatment of Growths Produced from Pruned Leaders.— The leader which was pruned during April or May must now be considered. Towards the top approximately four shoots will appear during the growing season. The uppermost is retained and tied in as the leading shoot. The remainder are pruned as soon as they have become half ripened. The time for this operation is generally about the middle of June. The shoots should then be about 12 to 15 inches long and about the thickness of a lead pencil. The pruning is exceptionally severe, and it is in this respect that Lorette's system differs so greatly from others. The shoots are cut right back to their base; that is to say, so that a stump of only $\frac{1}{4}$ inch remains. On this short piece of wood will be found the stipulary buds, which it is claimed are so easily converted into fruit-bearing laterals. In actual practice it will be found that many of these buds immediately start turning into fruit buds. Others produce darts, which, it will be remembered, are the intermediary stage between a bud and a fruit bud. On more vigorous trees the stipulary eyes may even produce the tree has been done during the summer months, therefore, and for this reason alone should commend itself.

I think perhaps it would be wise to repeat that both the Lorette and its modified form of pruning are suitable only for apples and pears.

CHAPTER TEN

PRUNING MISCELLANEOUS FRUITS

THE pruning of all fruits during the winter in which they were planted has been dealt with in the chapter devoted to that subject. The initial pruning is, of course, severe and often disturbing to the beginner, but is unquestionably essential to success. Fruits of the kinds described must be encouraged to grow strongly before there can be any thought of allowing them to bear fruit. This is the reason for the sound advice to buy young specimens of bush fruits. It is sometimes very difficult to build up satisfactory specimens from those which are transplanted as 'fruiting trees', because immediate fruiting after planting and satisfactory growth do not as a rule go hand in hand. It also follows that the most beneficial pruning cannot be applied to stunted trees.

Red and White Currants.—These fruit on old wood. The aim must be to build up a tree with five or six main branches, but the centre must always be kept well open. Short lateral growths must be spurred back to within three or four buds, and leaders should be cut back annually by half their length, always cutting to an outside bud. Great care must be exercised to leave no snags and to cut out all dead wood, in order to prevent the entrance of the Coral Spot fungus, which is particularly addicted to these fruits, and which, if once permitted to force an entrance, may gradually destroy the entire branch infected. The operation may be carried out in autumn, but in areas where birds are numerous and have a habit of attacking the buds it is frequently a good plan to delay pruning until spring.

When bushes of these fruits become very vigorous, as they frequently do, I think it is a good plan to summer prune. All young shoots except the leaders should be shortened so that they are left 4 to 5 inches long. The best time to do this is just before or as the fruit begins to colour.

Red and white currants, when grown as cordons, should

The variety *Lloyd George* can be treated as either a summer or an autumn fruiting raspberry. When grown, presumptively as the former, and after fruiting is over and pruning done, it will be found to fruit once more, in the autumn, on the tips of the shoots which were reserved for next year's fruit. This does not matter in the least, but it is wise to shorten back these tips when the second crop is finished.

Blackberries, etc.—Other berries, such as the loganberry, blackberry, Laxton berry, and Phenomenal berry, which are generally trained on wires, should have old fruiting wood removed when bearing is finished. The young wood which will produce next year's crop should then be tied in. Any shoots which are too long should not be 'tipped' until the following spring, otherwise secondary growth, which is not desirable, may be encouraged.

Peaches and Nectarines.—The method employed in pruning peaches and nectarines has been described in Chapter Three. The system may appear a trifle complicated at first, but is quite simple when carefully considered and put into practice. The following points should be thoroughly grasped:

Fruit is borne on one-year-old wood only.

All wood which is more than one year old is useless save for its purpose of forming a frame for the carrying of young wood.

Young wood which has fruited must be removed at the earliest possible moment consistent with certain practical points governed by the season of year.

Wood of current season's growth (which emanates from one-year-old wood or fruit-bearing wood) must be encouraged and carefully tied in beside older wood. It consists of the only available growth for next year's fruiting.

It is obvious that wood for next year's fruiting should be encouraged to grow from a point as low down on the current season's fruiting wood as possible. If this is done the minimum amount of old wood is left when one-year-old wood is cut and the young shoots tied in.

There is a danger that if trees are pruned in the autumn secondary growth may be encouraged. Pruning, or the cutting out of old fruiting wood, is consequently delayed until February. The young wood is then tied in.

Indoor Treatment.—It is usually the practice, after fruit has been gathered, to retain the foliage as long as possible in order to strengthen the wood. As soon as the leaves have dropped the old fruiting wood is cut away, and the young trained shoots are tied in.

Apricots.—The general pruning of apricots is similar to that recommended for peaches, the only difference being that the fruit in question will, unlike the latter, bear on old wood. The finest fruits are produced on one-year-old growths, and it is better to disbud and prune as suggested above. Spurs may be formed on older wood where necessary.

Apricots, peaches and nectarines are all subjects which are likely to require root pruning at some time or another, but more particularly when they are young. A careful look out must be exercised for excessive vigour, a sign that a check such as may be effected by judicious root pruning is necessary.

Plums.—*Standards.*—The initial treatment for newly planted standard plums should be the same as recommended for apples. Once the head of the tree is well formed, there should be little need for further pruning. A look out for excessive vigour should be maintained, however, especially during the first few years, and if strongly in evidence the tree should be lifted, root pruned and replanted. It is also as well during the first few seasons to pinch out the tips of particularly vigorous leaders. If this precaution is not taken, bare branches will result. Shoots more than 2 feet in length should be so treated during the growing months. In fact the best time for pruning standard plums is during June and July as at this season there is less chance of the silver leaf disease infection. When the trees are well established it may be found necessary from time to time to remove whole branches which are found to be crowding the centre. It may seem hard to do this when they may be covered with swelling fruits, but winter pruning should be avoided as far as possible, and it is better to sacrifice a single branch of fruit rather than lose the whole tree. Plums are most susceptible to this disease, and in districts where it is known to be present take no chances.

Fan-Trained.—The treatment for fan-trained trees is different. Young trees are sent out from nurseries provided fruit on spurs produced from the older wood, but the best produce comes from one-year-old wood.

When grown as a bush the Morello will be found to produce a lot of bare wood in the centre of the tree if it is left unpruned. This is because practically all fruit is borne on one-year-old wood and consequently each season this becomes further from the centre, leaving old wood behind with an occasional fruit bud here and there. In order to guard against this tendency, pinch out the growing tips of the most extended branches during June, and as soon as the fruit is picked thin out some of the older wood in much the same way as a black currant is pruned, but taking care not to remove too much young wood with the old, and making each cut either to a young shoot or to a dormant growth bud.

Hazel and Filbert.—These nuts are generally planted in gardens more for the purpose of screening than for production of quantities of fruit. In order to give of their best, bushes must have all their young shoots shortened by at least one-third of their length in order to encourage the production of laterals which bear the nuts. Laterals may be kept pinched to within 6 inches during the summer, and should again be spurred hard back in late winter, when the catkins, or male flowers, are withered. The cut should be made to a female flower-bud, which may be readily distinguished by its production of crimson styles at this period. It sometimes occurs that the shorter laterals bear female flowers terminally, in which case they should be left unpruned.

The Quince.—After a good head to the tree has been formed, as suggested for apples, very little pruning is necessary for the quince. Branches should be prevented from crossing at as early a period as possible, and overvigorous shoots should be checked by means of pinching.

The Walnut.—Walnuts require no pruning other than the supervision of the production of main branches. Any cutting back found to be necessary for this reason or removal of old damaged limbs should be done in September.

The Medlar.—Very little pruning can be done to medlar trees because their branches are so crooked and can never be relied upon to grow in any particular direction. It is wise to

Left: Pruning a standard plum tree with long-handled pruners. The work is being done in early summer to avoid danger of infection by silver leaf disease.

Right: The same tree after completion of pruning. Only crossing or overcrowded branches have been removed.

A section of a vine rod after correct winter pruning. Each side growth has been shortened to one or two buds.

Spring pinching of vine laterals to prevent unnecessary extension and a waste of energy.

make some provision to prevent boughs rubbing against one another.

The Mulberry.—The mulberry requires no pruning other than the attention suggested for walnuts.

Grape Vines.—In most establishments grape vines are grown on the spur system. That is to say, a single rod is treated with a view to ensure its becoming clothed with spurs throughout its length. These spurs give rise to shoots, which provide fruit, and in autumn are spurred hard back to a basal bud, which in turn produces next year's fruiting wood.

Treatment of a Young Rod.—A one-year-old grape vine purchased from the nursery should, after planting, be cut back to about 5 feet. The strongest leading shoot is tied in to form the continuation of the rod, whilst laterals are tied in horizontally. The leader should be stopped when it has made 5 feet of growth and afterwards allowed to grow at will. In the meantime the laterals, which will form the basis of fruit spurs, must be carefully watched. They must be thinned, and the strongest which remain must be so selected as to be arranged alternately on each side of the rod, and spaced at from 9 inches to 1 foot apart.

In autumn the laterals are spur pruned to one or two buds, and the leader shortened to 5 feet, making a total length of 10 feet for the entire rod.

The following spring resultant shoots from the spurs on the older part of the rod must be thinned to the single strongest, whilst the upper half of the rod is treated in a similar manner to that employed on the one-year-old portion the year previous. It is unwise to allow vines to carry fruit until they are three years old unless they are in exceptional vigour, and consequently all flower trusses should be pinched out at an early stage.

Treatment of an Established Rod.—Early pruning is important, and should be carried out as soon as all foliage has dropped. All shoots emanating from the spurs must be cut hard back to one or two buds. At the same time a careful watch must be kept for 'adventitious breaks', or young growths which sometimes appear from the older wood of a spur. If one of these is in evidence, the whole of the wood above it must be cut away, the aim being to keep spurs as short as possible, thus economising in glass space. It is obvious that

H

the older a spur becomes the more extended its formation, and every endeavour must be made to keep them short, not only by watching for adventitious breaks, but also by pruning hard back to the strongest basal bud every season.

Disbudding.—Vines invariably produce more shoots than are necessary. If the rod is well set with spurs at frequent intervals, there is no necessity for more than one shoot from each spur. Overcrowded shoots must be guarded against, as they not only weaken the rod, but also prevent thorough ripening of the strongest wood. All disbudding should be done at an early stage, so that shoots not required can be rubbed out with thumb and forefinger.

Stopping.—Each shoot must be stopped at two or three leaves beyond the flower truss. All sub-laterals—that is to say, side shoots produced from young growths—require attention. Those between the base of the young wood and the flower truss must be rubbed out at once. Those produced beyond the bunch must be stopped at one leaf. The aim at all times must be to fill the allotted space with leaves, and yet at the same time to prevent overcrowding.

Thinning the Bunches.—The number of bunches which a rod is allowed to carry varies with the size of the vine and also the weight of individual bunches. Generally speaking, from eight to twelve is a sufficient number. Remember that certain varieties, notably *Alnwick Seedling*, *Chasselas Napoleon* and *Canon Hall Muscat*, are bad setters, and ample time should be allowed to ascertain which bunches are likely to be the finest before thinning is done. Conversely, such varieties as *Bucklands Sweetwater*, *Lady Downs Seedling*, *Gros Colmar* and *Black Hamburgh*, are excellent setters, and their bunches may be thinned without anxiety.

Thinning the Fruits.—Varieties which set readily should have berries in the bunches thinned soon after the fruit is set, whilst those which do not set so readily should be watched for a week or so to observe which fruits are swelling. In thinning, the aim must be to remove more berries from the interior of the bunch than from the outer parts, for it is here that they are more likely to become overcrowded. The extent to which this operation should be done should be governed to some extent by the variety, but the aim in view must be not to allow berries to exert pressure upon one another when they are fully developed. Berries should not be touched by hand, and, besides special scissors, a thin piece of wood with a short fork at the end should be used with this object in view.

After the fruits have stoned they should again be looked over to see that there is no overcrowding. Some varieties, such as *Maddresfield Court, Lady Hutt* and *Foster's Seedling*, have a habit of splitting, and must be well thinned and a careful watch kept for the trouble. If it persists it is wiser to let the sub-laterals beyond the bunch grow on without stopping.

The Long-Rod System.—Some varieties, such as *Prince of Wales* and *Barbarossa*, do not respond well to the spur system, and are grown on what is termed the Long-Rod System. It is a method which may be employed for any variety, and may be depended upon to produce finer bunches than those obtained from rods devoted to spurring, although the number of bunches produced is smaller. Briefly the system is similar in general outline to that employed in peach cultivation. Whilst a young rod consisting of one-year-old wood is allowed to produce laterals which bear fruit, another young shoot is allowed to proceed from the base of the vine; and when the former has borne its fruit it is cut out, and the latter takes its place for the ensuing season.

The Extension System.—This consists of allowing one vine to fill an entire house. Training takes a considerable time, and it is suggested that the more satisfactory way of furnishing a house as a vinery is that of planting sufficient vines to be trained on the single-rod system.

Figs.—*Out of Doors.*—It has been said that a fig tree should never be pruned. This is probably true, for good results are sometimes obtained when trees are planted and left to themselves. Fruit is produced on young wood. In very favourable localities fruit borne on the current season's wood may reach maturity during the year, but for the most part it is the smallest fruits produced at the extremities of such wood which ripen during the following summer.

Figs must never be allowed to grow luxuriantly and should not be fed until their fruit has freely set and begins to swell.

Indoors.—This fruit has been grown as a fan-trained specimen under glass, but by far the most satisfactory method is to grow them as bushes in pots. A young tree supplied with a single shoot should have the basal 6 inches disbudded to form a short stem. If growth is vigorous stop at about four leaves beyond the disbudded portion. Shoots will then break and form the foundation of the bush. If these laterals are weak they must be tipped, and next year side growths will be produced. All subsequent growths must be stopped at five or six leaves, the sole aim being to build up a compact branching tree with no bare stems.

CHAPTER ELEVEN

HEDGES AND TOPIARY SPECIMENS

HEDGE-MAKING plants may be divided into two classes. These are those, such as the yew, holly, box and cypress, which should be bushy and well furnished down to the ground level. There is little need to cut such subjects at all during the first season following planting. On the other hand, there are other subjects, such as privet, hornbeam, beech and hawthorn, which are much quicker growing, and which repay a good heading back shortly after planting in order to encourage them to break and become bushy from the base.

Treatment for the first season, then, can be summed up as follows: Slow growing subjects which are in full vigour and are well furnished require very little trimming the first year, save for the removal here and there of vigorous shoots which are obviously misplaced. Quick-growing subjects which are but one or two seasons old when planted must be hard cut back shortly after planting in order to encourage thickness from the base upwards.

A few words on that much-discussed hedge plant, *Lonicera nitida*, may not be out of place here. It is a very useful plant where a hedge not more than 5 or 6 feet in height is required. But until it is finally planted in a permanent position it must be transplanted every year without fail, on account of its coarse rooting habit when left undisturbed. Consequently it is strongly recommended that one-year-old plants only be planted for hedge-making, unless a definite guarantee is given that the stock has been regularly transplanted every year. Unfortunately, this is not always carried out by a great number of nurserymen, with the result that bushes are sent out by some which are not only straggly but also have very little fibre underground. In consequence they transplant badly and present a very sorry appearance.

Frequent occurrence of this has unfortunately earned this excellent shrub a bad name in many districts. The only treatment for such plants is hard heading back, with the result that the gardener would have done just as well, if not better, by purchasing one-year-old stock. Although *Lonicera nitida* is fairly vigorous, well-grown plants are sufficiently bushy not to require heading back during the first year, but owing to its spreading habit attention must be given to the sides of the hedge, which must not be allowed to grow outside the allotted space.

Slow Growing Hedges.—Necessity for the removal of much top growth is rare. Vigorous young shoots, which take the lead and grow more strongly than others, should be curbed by lightly clipping them, or, alternatively, they may be pinched out. More attention is required at the sides, and care should be taken to see that no energy is wasted in the form of strong, outward growth. Clipping should be done at least twice in the season, the first being sufficiently late not to encourage strong premature growth in spring, and the last sufficiently early in autumn to allow resultant growth to ripen thoroughly before the first frosts. Generally speaking, from May until August inclusive is a safe period for the operations. Within reason, the more frequent the clipping the finer will be the hedge.

Quick Growing Hedges.—Such hedges are best trimmed at the same time as recommended for the previous section. No harm, however, is done by carrying out the work in the winter months upon such hardy subjects as privet and hawthorn. Beech and hornbeam carry their dead leaves until the spring, and, for this reason, are usually left until May. The first trimming should always consist of a heavy heading back of the topmost growths in order to maintain a bushy habit, whilst at the same time the sides must be attended to at least twice during the growing season.

Topiary and Formal Specimens.—Topiary and formal specimens should be trimmed twice a year, in May and July. Care must be exercised not to cut into old wood. If this is done the shape may be spoiled, and it may take some time before the matter can be adjusted. Regular attention is the first essential, and the operator must always exercise patience, for hurried work with the clippers may in a few minutes do damage which it will take years to rectify.

CHAPTER TWELVE

CALENDAR OF PRUNING OPERATIONS

It is a great mistake to lay down hard-and-fast rules as to dates for the carrying out of any particular gardening operation. Climatic conditions are so variable that no prearranged programme should be accepted as any more than an approximate guide.

The following calendar should be of some assistance as indicating the normal period during which various pruning operations should be carried out. I have purposely omitted flowering shrubs, since the correct date for pruning each of these subjects may be readily identified in the Reference List of Shrubs.

January

Fruit.—Prune apples, pears, plums and cherries (fan-trained), quinces, gooseberries, currants (red and white), blackcurrants (newly planted bushes only), raspberries (autumn fruiting varieties), peaches and nectarines (out of doors).

Flowers.—Clematis of *Viticellæ*, *Jackmanii*, *aramaticæ*, *erectæ* and *wokingensis* types may be pruned.

February

Fruit.—Continue work with fruits as recommended for January.

Cut back newly planted raspberries to 6 inches.

Disbud shoots on grape vines under glass.

Spur back laterals on cob nuts as soon as catkins have withered.

March

Fruit.—Complete pruning of fruits as recommended for January.

Thin berries of early grapes.

Start disbudding peaches and nectarines (indoors).

Tip back unripened shoots of raspberries, gooseberries and blackberries.

Flowers.—Thin shoots of strong growing herbaceous plants to get best results.

Make a start on bush and standard roses towards the end of the month.

Clip ivy.

April

Fruit.—Remove blossoms from young strawberry plants except those planted prior to or during previous August. Treat similarly all crowns intended for propagation (i.e. for runner Production this year). Destroy 'blind' plants at the same time.

Attend to necessary pruning of sweet cherries.

Stop shoots of grapes two joints beyond bunches.

Flowers.—Complete pruning of bush and standard roses.

Attend to stopping decorative and single chrysanthemums.

May

Fruit.—Pinch back strong shoots on wall-trained trees.

Continue stopping shoots of vines and disbudding peaches.

Thin fruits of gooseberries.

Remove raspberry suckers unless required for propagation.

Flowers.—Trim hedges and topiary specimens.

Give ivy second and final trimming.

Thin shoots of herbaceous plants.

June

Fruit.—Summer prune red and white currants, apricots and plums on walls. Cut out surplus branches of standard plums.

Flowers.—Stop outdoor chrysanthemums.

Remove faded blossoms of annuals. Also pyrethrums and lupins.

July

Fruit.—Summer prune apples and pears.

Thin shoots of Morello cherries.

Restrict numbers of strawberry runners.
Thin apples, pears and plums.
Flowers.—Remove seed pods of annuals and bedding plants.
Trim back delphiniums and lupins which have finished flowering.
Clip evergreen hedges.
Prune rambler roses as soon as flowering is over.
Summer prune bush and standard roses.

August

Fruit.—Complete summer pruning of apples and pears.
Cut out old fruiting wood of raspberries and loganberries.
Summer prune hazel and cob nuts.
Flowers.—Complete pruning of rambler roses.
Disbud chrysanthemums.

September

Fruit.—Cut out old fruiting wood of blackberries.
Prune black currants.
Remove large fruit from outdoor figs which are too late to ripen, leaving the small ones for next year's crop.

October

Fruit.—Where early crops of grapes, peaches and nectarines are produced by forcing treatment, the vines and trees should now be reaching the resting stage and may, consequently, be pruned.
Flowers.—Cutting away dead stems of herbaceous plants is a task for this month, but refrain from cutting green, sappy growths.

November

Fruit.—As soon as leaves have fallen from apple and pear trees, currants and gooseberries, pruning may be started.
Ornamental Trees.—Where lopping of main trunks or

large branches is necessary this is a suitable month for the operation.

December

The balance of last month's work may be completed when weather permits.

INDEX

Abelia, 52, 63
Abutilon, 63
Acacia, 63
Acers, 63
Adhesive tape for bark ringing, 32
Æsculus, 63
Ailanthus, 63
Akebia, 63
Amelanchier, 63
American blight (woolly aphis), 19
Ampelopsis, 63
Anchusa, 22
Andromeda, 52
Annual chrysanthemum, 24
  lupin, 24
Antirrhinum, 16
Apples, 43–4, 81–98
  aged fruit spurs, 87
  biennial bearing, 88–9
  brown rot, 85
  bush trees, 90–1
    pruning of, 85
  canker, 19, 84–5
  cordons, 27, 92–5
    from maidens, 93
    increasing vigour, 81–2
    suitable varieties, 94–5
    summer pruning, 95
    winter pruning, 96
  dehorning, 90
  dwarf pyramids, 96
    from maidens, 97–8
  espaliers, pruning of, 95–6
  leaders, 88
  maiden trees, 90
    cordons from, 93
    dwarf pyramids from, 97–8
  nicking to encourage or dis-
    courage growth of bud, 90
  pruning, bush trees, 85
    for shape, 83
    root, 27–9
    summer, 92
    to give light and air, 83
    transplanted trees, 91
  removal of dead and diseased
    wood, 84
  standard trees, 92

Apples, tip fruiting varieties, 89
  treatment after continuous hard
    pruning, 85–7
  varieties disposed to biennial
    bearing, 88
  vigour control, 81
Apricots, 109
Aralia, 63
Arbutus, 54, 63
Arundinaria, 63
Atriplex, 63
Aucuba, 52, 63
Azalea, 24, 59
Azara, 52, 64

Bamboo (Phyllostachys), 67
Bark, blistering and cracking of, 19
Bartonia, 24
Bedding plants, 23
Beech, 117
Berberis, 52, 55, 64
Blackberries, 41, 106, 108
Bladder senna (Colutea), 64
Blistering of bark, 19
Blotches on leaves, 19
Box, 117
Branches, ingrowing, 83
Brindles, 100, 102
Broom (Cytisus), 59, 65
Brown rot, 85
Buckthorn (Hippophæ), 66
Budding, 25
Buddleia, 52, 64
Bulbs, preventing seed formation,
  24
Burning dead or diseased wood, 85

Callicarpa, 64
Calluna (heather), 64
Calycanthus, 64
Camellias, 64
Canker, 19, 84–5
  effects of, 18–19
Carnation, 21, 22
Carpentaria, 64
Caryopteris, 64
Cassinia, 64
Ceanothus, 53, 64

123